REDISCOVERING

JESUS'

PRIORITIES

LEONARD DOOHAN

REFLECTIONS ON CONTEMPORARY SPIRITUALITY FOR CHRISTIAN ADULTS

Copyright 2014, Leonard Doohan
All rights reserved.

The Catholic Edition of the Revised Standard Version of the Bible, copyright 1989, 1993 by the Division of Christian Education of the National Council of the Churches of Christ in the United States of America. Used by permission. All rights reserved.

ISBN-13: 978-0991006731

ISBN-10: 0991006739

REDISCOVERING JESUS' PRIORITIES

Table of Contents

INTRODUCTION 1

THREE GIFTS 7
    LOVE—in unloving times 8
        The Father's great gift is love
        Jesus makes love visible among us
        Love is the essence of our discipleship
        Practical consequences of this priority
    FAITH—when doubt prevails 15
        In faith we are taught by God
        Believe in him whom God has sent
        Our journey of faith
        Consequences of commitment to faith
    HOPE—when all seems hopeless 21
        In hope we are saved
        Jesus proclaimed God's gift of hope
        We live in hope
        Present consequences of living in hope

THREE CHALLENGES 29
    CONVERSION—in times of self-righteousness 30
        Called to conversion
        Discovering the values of God
        Conversion is a process
        Contemporary components of conversion
    INTEGRITY—when we have lost respect for truth. 36
        Jesus' principles of integrity
        The quest for integrity
        Practices of integrity
    LIFE IN THE SPIRIT—when others mock transcendent values 41
        Disciples search for fulfillment
        Some key aspects of contemporary spirituality
        Some practical aspects of contemporary spirituality

THREE SUPPORTS **49**
    COMMUNITY—when self-interest prevails **50**
        Jesus calls his followers to build community
        Characteristics of the Christian community
        Community as a contemporary support of faith
    **SHARED MINISTRY—when many are so
self-centered** **55**
        Companions who share in mission and ministry
        A theology of ministry
        Shared ministry in our contemporary world
    **UNIVERSALITY—when we fear diversity
and stifle dissent** **61**
        Jesus' example of accepting everyone
        Our discipleship means being open to all
        A spirituality of universality

**ONE GOAL: TRANSFORMATION—when we seek
    control** **69**
        The goal of transformation
        Our response to the gift of transformation
        Results of this transformation

INTRODUCTION

Periodically in life we assess our priorities and measure them to our actions. What we say is important can simply be words if not followed by change in life-style, decisions, and attitudes. While our priorities can be lofty ideals, most often they are down to earth practical endeavors that will concretely affect daily life and relationships as well as our personal long-term well being. In fact, it might be a good exercise at this point to make a list of our priorities, maybe in five or six areas. Are they expansive or mundane, lofty or practical, self-centered or other oriented, culturally limiting or universal, virtuous or secular, tied to tradition or future oriented? When we look at them, are they long term priorities of life or simply short term strategies? Do these priorities include the religious and spiritual dimensions of our lives?

I doubt that Jesus completed this kind of an exercise before beginning his public ministry but priorities did emerge in his life, preaching and ministry. They seemed to bypass the ordinary emphases of our daily lives and work. They seemed to be idealistic, courageous, challenging, and transformational. His priorities became evident in the daily situations of his life as he made decisions to heal on the Sabbath, to have contact with a leper, to generously respond to human need, to confront false priorities of his day, to challenge failed leadership, and to view reality from a different spiritual perspective. Jesus' priorities were focused on other people, on societal changes, on transformation, and how we direct our lives to God.

Just before Jesus entered Jerusalem and faced the events that led to his passion, a group of Greeks asked to meet with him. Jesus welcomed this encounter as a sign of the future growth that would come to the Church through his passion and death, endured for love of humanity and for its salvation and transformation. However, knowing the fickleness of the uncommitted, Jesus was troubled and spoke to the crowd. "The light is with you for a little longer. Walk while you have the light, so that the darkness may not overtake you. If you walk in the darkness, you do not know where you are going. While you have the light, believe in the light, so that you may become children of light" (John 12:35-36). Earlier in his ministry, when asked to explain the parable of the sower to his disciples, Jesus took occasion to comment on the lack of understanding and commitment he saw in many people. "For this people's heart has grown dull, and their ears are hard of hearing, and they have shut their eyes; so that they might not look with their eyes, and listen with their ears, and understand with their heart and turn— and I would heal them" (Matthew 13:15). In every generation we see many who lack understanding of Jesus' message, others who choose to live in darkness, and still others who turn their hearts away from the values Jesus came to teach.

Our own generation is no different than others. When we look at ourselves and our Christian churches today we hardly seem to pursue the same priorities that Jesus pursued. Even if we leave aside—which we should not—the sexual, financial, and social misconduct and cover-ups of our Church officials, we still remain appropriately shocked and baffled that the primary focus of many Church officials and members remains issues of sexual, procreative, and conjugal life. In fact, many issues given prominence by contemporary Christian officials and groups are ones Jesus never dealt with at all, even though those same problems existed in his time. They are not unimportant, but they are not the key priorities that Jesus' teachings call for. When we look at Christianity's self-portrayal today, we can ask ourselves "Did Jesus come and die merely for this?"

The evangelist Matthew had an interesting perspective on Jesus' coming and message, when he described both as "an earthquake" (Matthew 8:24; 21:10; 27:52; 28:2). He reminds us all as disciples that we cannot become paralyzed with fear or helplessness, for the coming of the Lord Jesus and the challenge he brings form part of the most earth-shattering event of all time. In Luke's gospel Jesus said he had come to set the world on fire with enthusiasm for his message (Luke 12:49). Mark tells us that when

Jesus spoke the crowd was spellbound at his teaching (Mark 6:2). It is difficult today to be spellbound by the teachings we hear in our Churches from our fellow Christians. They certainly do not set us on fire with enthusiasm, let alone the world, and they are nothing like an earth-shattering event. What has happened? Why are the current priorities of some Christians and especially Church officials out of sync with Jesus'?

Jesus told us his teachings could remove the burdens of life and bring refreshment to our spirit (Matthew 11:28-30). In the Beatitudes he proclaimed that his teachings would make adherents truly happy (Matthew 5:3-12). He insisted his teachings were the antithesis of, and went beyond, any previous teachings of other religious leaders (Matthew 5:21-48). He also warned that followers need to focus on essentials and leave aside the traditions of the elders (Matthew 15:1-20). Finally he gave a quick guide to authenticity—a tree is known by its fruits (Matthew 12:34). We should ask ourselves which priorities of Jesus achieve all this for us. Unfortunately, many today both outside and inside the Church no longer find it a community with a vision that leads to concrete living circumstances that portray Jesus' priorities. It does not reflect the consciousness and value system of the historical Jesus. He anticipated that some would abandon the priorities of his message and said that for others their love would just grow cold (Matthew 24:12). Of course, situations change over time, and new issues come to the fore that Christians should address, while making sure they reflect the mind and emphases of Jesus. Much of what we see and hear today has no direct foundation in Scripture. When all is said and done, Jesus knew what he wanted, articulated his values very clearly, and had a sophisticated understanding of the priorities that he was convinced would transform the world. There is a wholeness and wholesomeness about his integrated vision.

It is critical that we rediscover his priorities and live them faithfully, as we deal with the new challenges of our times. Luke recounts an interesting story about a man who wanted to become a disciple of Jesus. He tells Jesus that he would first like to have the time to bury his father. Now, clearly the man's father has not just died. He would hardly be out in the fields listening to a travelling public speaker if his father had just died. Rather, he would be at home—like Martha and Mary were—receiving friends and family in the long bereavement required in those times. It is very likely that the man's father was standing beside him, proud of his son. The man is telling Jesus that he wants to stay home for as long as it takes so that when his father eventually dies he can fulfill the obligations required of him as eldest son. Only then will he be ready to become a disciple. He is promising a commitment when he has taken care of everything else. Nowadays, such a half-hearted disciple wants to take care to set up a family, establish a good career, become financially secure, and so on, before dedicating himself or herself to Jesus. Discipleship does not wait. Let all of us reassess our lives and recommit ourselves to the priorities of Jesus when we hear his call.

Discipleship in every generation means making Jesus' priorities our own and reproducing these realities in our own time. We find these priorities in Scripture which becomes a source of knowledge, inspiration, and edification. It is also an inspired synthesis and vision, a measuring rod of authentic spirituality, and a blueprint that calls us to life. However, Jesus' great discourses to his disciples were not only for their benefit but essentially present them with what they are to pass on to others. By the time we read the gospels we already have a history of these diverse communities, each trying to live faithfully Jesus' message. Mark's community was passing through times of crisis and uncertainty. Matthew's was a fairly affluent city community trying to sort out its relationship with Judaism. Luke's was adapting the message for a Gentile and well-educated community. John's was more interested in proclaiming the Jesus of the Church's present and future. Jesus is a multidimensional figure for the early Church, and each community struggled to live his priorities in changing times. The Church throughout the centuries has dedicated itself to Scripture's presentation of Jesus' message, as we see in Church history, the lives of the mystics, the sense of the faithful, and the varieties of spiritualities. In some periods the Church has been successful and in others not so.

A new spirit is stirring in the Church. We must overcome the failures of the past and prepare ourselves for a future of growth and responsibility. While many have left the institutional churches, and sadly may never return, perhaps the challenge to renewal of Pope Francis may re-attract them to the essentials of Christian commitment. As an antidote to all we have lost by emphasizing secondary issues, we need a fresh commitment to the priorities of

Jesus. Let us rekindle spiritual insight, accept our spiritual destiny, and refocus on the essential teaching of salvation. As we look at Jesus' message, we can eliminate the boundaries between then and now and live the gospel with new enthusiasm today. The central section of Marks' gospel opens and closes with two stories of the healings of blind men. This technique of bracketing a section of narrative—in this case Jesus' journey to Jerusalem—with two similar stories emphasizes the author's conviction that the central idea of his narrative is that Jesus comes to heal our blindness. It is not that we are completely blind—the first blind man finds that people look like trees and are not in focus for him. Rather we need to see more clearly what often we only see partially. During the journey to Jerusalem in Mark's gospel Jesus clarifies for the apostles what are the central priorities of his message, and it is our calling to see them more clearly. As we discover the deep meaning of these priorities we can live them more faithfully. Then these priorities can impact our own times as we transform what we see into what we would never have imagined.

THREE GIFTS

Jesus summarized the purpose of his coming very powerfully when he said, "I came that they may have life, and have it abundantly" (John 10:10). To help us achieve this he gave us three fundamental energies of the soul that would become source values of life and guiding values for all we do. With these three gifts he gave us new life, a new spirit, and a new way of making judgments in everything we do (Ezekiel 37:1-14). When we think about love, faith, and hope we are not referring to our virtues, practices, or devotions but to three God-given powers that transform our lives. We call these three gifts theological virtues because they come from God.

As Christians we understand that what we do is not as important as what God is doing in us. Unfortunately, a lot of people follow blindly, with limited intellectual knowledge of God in their minds, with accumulations of many small loves in their souls, and with misguided hope in their hearts. Rather, we must let God love in and through us, believe in and through us, and hope in and through us. Instead of focusing our affections on multiple objects, we need to leave them all aside and let God's love flow through us. Instead of accumulating our knowledge of God from every source imaginable, we leave it all aside and let God teach us about divine life in faith. Instead of appreciating God's gifts to us by remembering everything done in the past, we leave it all aside and let God fill us with hope for the future. These three gifts of love, faith, and hope are three of Jesus' great priorities.

LOVE—in unloving times

The most important priority in Jesus' life and teachings is to convey to every person how much God loves everyone. Jesus came to the world filled with the Father's love in order to share that love with each of us. However, our world is rapidly becoming a loveless place, and we Christians have to change that by making this priority of Jesus our own.

The Father's great gift is love.

The evangelist John tells us that early in Jesus' ministry, after the call of the twelve apostles, Jesus went up to Jerusalem for the feast of the Passover. While there a Pharisee, a teacher of the Law, came to visit him. He was interested in Jesus and his vision of life but afraid lest other Pharisees should see his devotion, and so he visited Jesus at night hoping that no one would see him. Jesus explained to Nicodemus God's plan for the world and the reason for Jesus' own mission. Both points focus on the need to present to the world God's strategy of love. "For God so loved the world that he gave his only Son, so that everyone who believes in him may not perish but may have eternal life" (John 3:16). Jesus makes it clear that the point of departure for men and women in their search for and appreciation of God is God's love for the world and not their love for God. Jesus came to reveal God's reign of love for all and to make us all aware that we are children of a loving God. He came to the world God loves, filled with enduring love, to give us all a share in that love. The writer of the First Letter of John had reflected on these things and presents a powerful summary. "Beloved, let us love one another, because love is from God; everyone who loves is born of God and knows God. Whoever does not love does not know God, for God is love" (1 John 4:7-8). The Trinity consists in the mutual sharing of love by the three persons, and the Incarnation is the extension of that love to the world. The whole of salvation history is summed up in love, the greatest priority in Jesus' ministry. He did not come to give us endless rules and regulations nor to threaten us with punishment should we fail. He had one great priority in his coming, to reveal to the world the importance of love. God's being and purpose is love, God's gift is love, Jesus is the incarnation of love, and our response is to let this love permeate our lives. "God's love was revealed among us in this way: God sent his only Son into the world so that we might live through him. In this is love, not that we loved God but that he loved us and sent his Son to be the atoning sacrifice for our sins" (1 John 4:9-10).

All religion is the linking of two realms of life, our present one and a life beyond this one that gives meaning to our existence in this one. We cannot bridge the chasm between these two realms of life without God's help and that comes through revelation, in which God tells us how life ought to be lived. If we do not hear, or see, or understand this, we lose our way. Our understanding of God and God's will is vital for our individual and communal lives. We are not making an effort-filled journey to God but being drawn by God towards the divine life of love. The Scriptures present God as almighty and powerful, insisting that God is Sovereign Lord who has a plan for the world and directs the unfolding of every step in this plan. However, God is also Father and Savior, filled with concern and compassion for all men and women. The emphasis on God as Father (184 times in the New Testament) shows the intimate, loving relationship of God towards all men and women. God is all goodness, dwells among us, is life-giving, knows what we need, and lovingly takes care of us. God is ever present, always ready to help us in our needs, and is constantly and lovingly involved in our growth. "God lives in us, and his love is perfected in us" (1 John 4:12). This is not the usual portrait of God found in world religions, but the Christian revelation is different in so far as it centers on love.

Religion's role is to focus believers' dedication on the essentials of revelation and for the most part it does a reasonably good job of this in many periods of history. But religion is not always correct in its emphases, and Jesus spent much of his time challenging religious leaders of his day because of their belief in their own schemes and ideas rather than in the priorities of revelation. Would Jesus be happy with many of today's religious leaders and their priorities? I think not!

Jesus makes love visible among us.

God's revelation concerning the centrality of love is faithfully brought to completion through Jesus, himself the Beloved of the Father. The eternal purpose of God is made real in Jesus' life and ministry. He alone places us in contact with the will of God—he is not just a messenger but *the* messenger. He fulfills our hopes and aspirations, assuring us of peace, happiness, the loving care of God, and salvation offered to all. He brings us healing, purification, and compassion in God's name. He teaches us the ways and the will of God. He binds us to each other by building unity and reconciliation. As Emmanuel, he calls us to God and reveals God as a loving Father. So, Jesus comes from the Father with signs and wonders as his credentials, and he proclaims God's love for the world. The Father loves the Son (John 3:35), hands over everything to him and now works through Jesus who claims, "I do as the Father has commanded me, so that the world may know that I love the Father" (John 14:31); and "I have kept my Father's commandments and abide in his love" (John 15:10). In fact, Jesus says, "My teaching is not mine but his who sent me" (John 7:16). The relationship between Jesus and the Father is so intimate that Jesus can say, the Father loves the Son, has personally sent him to the world, and "Whoever has seen me has seen the Father" (John 14:9).

Jesus' message focuses primarily on the life of love that the Father wants for the world. The Father loves the world so much that he offers his only Son whom he loves for its salvation. Jesus can even say that the Father and he are one. Having spent eternity in the mutual love of the Trinity, the Father extends this love to the world through the Son, through whom the Father shows the world the depth of his salvific love. Jesus becomes the incarnation of the authority, power, and love of God. It is an extraordinary religious revelation, so powerful it becomes a motive for the disciples' reflection and conversion. The Father has unlimited love for humanity and Jesus focuses on revealing this as one of his great priorities. The writer of the letter to the Ephesians brilliantly sums up the gift of God's love that we encounter in Jesus. "Blessed be the God and Father of our Lord Jesus Christ, who has blessed us in Christ with every spiritual blessing in the heavenly places . . . . With all wisdom and insight he has made known to us the mystery of his will, according to his good pleasure that he set forth in Christ, as a plan for the fullness of time, to gather up all things in him, things in heaven and things on earth" (Ephesians 1:3, 8-10).

Before Jesus' departure from this world, he assured his followers of God's continued loving presence to them and of the importance of their commitment to a life based on love. "I will not leave you orphaned; I am coming to you. In a little while the world will no longer see me, but you will see me; because I live, you also will live. On that day you will know that I am in my Father, and you in me, and I in you. They who have my commandments and keep them are those who love me; and those who love me will be loved by my Father, and I will love them and reveal myself to them." (John 14:18-21). Having taught them how much the Father loves them, Jesus also assures his followers of his personal love and guarantees that it will continue. "And I will ask the Father, and he will give you another Advocate, to be with you forever. This is the Spirit of truth, whom the world cannot receive, because it neither sees him nor knows him. You know him, because he abides with you, and he will be in you" (John 14:16-17). Thus, the Spirit, the Paraclete, becomes the principle of new life for believers, their sanctifier, and their teacher and guide. He will always be with them, for God "gives the Spirit without measure" (John 3:34).

Love is the essence of our discipleship.

The gospel writers insist that the disciples' commitment to holiness should be expressed in love (Matthew 5:44-48). This was Jesus' own way of fidelity to his Father throughout his ministry. Jesus placed love in the list of the ten commandments and made it equal to love of God. "On these two commandments hang all the law and the prophets" (Matthew 22:40). He placed love above worship and above the Sabbath commandment. Jesus not only understood love as greater than any other individual command or practice, but as the embodiment of the spirit of all. Towards the end of the Sermon on the Mount, he summed up his teachings: "In everything do to others as you would have them do to you; for this is the law and the prophets" (Matthew 7:12). In his sermon on the final judgment Jesus insisted that everyone's talents should be used for the benefit of others and that everyone will be judged by their love for others especially the needy. In an interesting section Jesus insists that the love he wants from his disciples needs to be qualitatively better than that suggested by teachings prior to him (Matthew 5:43-48).

The new goal of Christianity is universal love—treating others with respect, benevolence, unconditional love, and universal concern. The model for all Christians is the Father's extraordinary love for humanity. "But love your enemies, do good, and lend, expecting nothing in return. Your reward will be great, and you will be children of the Most High; for he is kind to the ungrateful and the wicked. Be merciful, just as your Father is merciful. Do not judge, and you will not be judged; do not condemn, and you will not be condemned. Forgive, and you will be forgiven; give, and it will be given to you" (Luke 6:35-38). In John's gospel Jesus takes this challenge to model our lives on the Father's love a step further. "As the Father has loved me, so I have loved you; abide in my love" (John 15:9). Three times Jesus tells the disciples that if they love him they will keep his commandments—commands that enhance life in the human community.

Before his departure to return to his Father, Jesus gives his disciples a new commandment. "I give you a new commandment, that you love one another. Just as I have loved you, you also should love one another. By this everyone will know that you are my disciples, if you have love for one another" (John 13:34-35). The union between the Father and Jesus is the model for the disciples union with Jesus and with each other. "As the Father has loved me, so I have loved you; abide in my love" (John 15:9). Abiding in Jesus' love is the ongoing life of disciples who become like branches united to the life-giving vine. Then they receive Jesus' word, the Father's protection from evil, and the pledge of union with Jesus in eternity. Jesus gives his life for those who are truly his. In fact, he nourishes their abiding union with his own flesh (John 6:56). All these disciples who are Jesus' own have received a transforming gift of new life, and actively respond to the gift. Jesus' hope for them is always the same, that they be transformed by the Father's love—"that the love with which you have loved me may be in them, and I in them" (John 17:26). Thus, God's strategy of love is clear—the Father, Son, Spirit, and disciples dwell in each other because of the love they share which is the very life of God.

The fact that love is Jesus' greatest priority leads to important consequences for all disciples. Jesus spoke about water, bread, and light, saying they were life-giving. However, beyond these teachings lies the conviction that if you have love you are living, and if you do not you are already dead. When a lawyer asked what he had to do to have eternal life, the answer was simple, clear, and blunt—love. This love is critical for salvation, and Jesus not only emphasizes gentleness, compassion, and mutual service, but he can also be very strong, sharp, and even violent where the lack of love is concerned. He was not opposed to telling some loveless individuals "You are already condemned." He declared that some people always love the darkness which covers their infidelity. To others he warned "You do not have the love of God in you." His words to the Pharisees remain a condemnation that no religious leader can ever forget. Perhaps one of the saddest moments was when Jesus acknowledged "And because of the increase of lawlessness, the love of many will grow cold" (Matthew 24:12).

Practical consequences of this priority of Jesus.

Consumerism has corrupted our world and even our spirituality. We always want more of everything—whether objects, experiences, position, people's praise, and so on. We have so many objects that we claim to love and need. The first priority Jesus gives us in his life and teachings is to love God and one's neighbor above all else. We cannot disperse the power of our love among endless secondary objects. Rather, we focus the full strength of our love on God alone and on our neighbors as signs of God's presence among us. Much of what we want and claim to love can only be ours at other people's expense. Comparing ourselves to others—their position, salary, the praise they receive, their promotions, and so on, always leads us away from love.

An important part of every day is that we make decisions based always on what is the most loving thing to do. This takes time, self-training, and discernment. It means evaluating every decision we need to make and seeing the pros and cons of each one, asking ourselves which decisions would lead to harm and which would lead to good, harmony, and love. At first, this will take a lot of time but with practice it becomes almost spontaneous. However, it is through our decisions that we manifest our values and Jesus' priorities. Consequently this is a practice worth fostering.

Reconciliation is an integral part of the lives of those who give priority to love. Our world today desperately needs a spirit of ongoing reconciliation in friendships, families, political discussion, national vision, and international endeavors. Our world is polarized like never before. St. Paul considered reconciliation to be the very essence of the Christian message, and if we want to pursue the priority of love in all we do then we must become reconciling people.

Love starts in community and is part of all our efforts to build unity and community today. Community requires real and reciprocal relationships and members build up strong communities with simple expressions of humanity, care, trust, and support. It also needs creative tolerance of differences, solidarity, and peacemaking. All groups have their own stages in psychological development and members will need to respect these different stages, and Christians will need to channel the group through its positive and painful growth stages.

Maintaining the priority of love requires constant evaluation. This vision of love is important, a matter of life and death. Jesus calls disciples to decide what kind of people they want to become. Will we build our lives on the love that Jesus taught or will we give ourselves to non-love? There is nothing in-between. This is the most essential decision of life. Love is the norm for judging Christian character. The world, each of us, can respond to the challenge of the "undreamed of possibility of love" (Luis Segundo) or choose a world of selfishness and hatred.

LOVE

The essence of Christianity is love. God is love. The Trinity lives in mutual love. The Incarnation is part of God's strategy of love. Jesus exemplifies and teaches love. Disciples are called to individual and communal love. The Church's mission is to portray love to the world.

Questions for personal reflection or group discussion.
1. Is love the center and most important aspect of your life?
2. Is your image of God based primarily on love? Explain how you think about these issues.
3. Why do you think Jesus came to this world? Explain his purpose in your own words.

4. Can you give examples of how you made decisions this week based on what you saw as the most loving thing to do?
5. What are the practical consequences for you of this priority of Jesus?

FAITH-when doubt prevails

Faith is a way of knowing God and the life God wants for us. No one knows God by accumulating knowledge, information, intellectual insight, but only by abandoning whatever knowledge we previously had and journeying in darkness and unknowing, letting God be our teacher and guide. We know God more through faith than we do through the accumulation of knowledge. We can earn the latter through our own achievements, but not the former—that is complete gift from God.

In faith we are taught by God.

Jesus tells us that the Father makes this gift to us, teaching us a new way to journey in life. "It is written in the prophets, 'And they shall all be taught by God.' Everyone who has heard and learned from the Father comes to me" (John 6:45). This gift of faith is not a static concept but a dynamic one that implies active commitment to Jesus and the life he sets before us. Faith is not a single act—it is a basic characteristic of Christian personality, and as disciples we live in a different way as a result of this gift. With the gift of faith, God works unceasingly to draw us through Jesus to divine life. Belief in God is made manifest by belief in Jesus who made this clear while preaching in Jerusalem. "Whoever believes in me believes not in me but in him who sent me. And whoever sees me sees him who sent me. I have come as light into the world, so that everyone who believes in me should not remain in the darkness" (John 12:44-46). Again, during the Last Supper, Jesus reaffirms this unique relationship between believing in him and believing in the Father. "Do not let your hearts be troubled. Believe in God, believe also in me" (John 14:1).

Faith is an inner knowledge, experience and communication that produces a life-giving vision of God, a different kind of knowledge based on emptying oneself and being filled with God's new way of seeing life. It produces the typical aspects of discipleship as seen in the Sermon on the Mount—a recognition of God, authenticity, spiritual integrity, inner recollection, genuine piety, and awareness of the end of life. God offers faith as a gift that one can receive or not. But there are serious consequences. Belief means acceptance, light, becoming Jesus' own, being children of God, whereas unbelief means rejection, darkness, belonging to the world, and being children of Evil. Jesus draws a clear conclusion concerning this choice. "Very truly, I tell you, anyone who hears my word and believes him who sent me has eternal life, and does not come under judgment, but has passed from death to life" (John 5:24). Later, he expresses these same ideas but in more detail. "Everything that the Father gives me will come to me, and anyone who comes to me I will never drive away; for I have come down from heaven, not to do my own will, but the will of him who sent me" (John 6:37-38).

So, faith is one of Jesus' priorities. He affirms that it is a gift of the Father, who draws us to himself and helps us persevere in our commitment. Believing is a personal choice, the human response to the loving and welcoming gift of the Father—this response is a believing obedience and a loving interpersonal relationship with Jesus. Believing is a new birth that results in a continuous dialogue between the disciple and God—the former empty of previous knowledge and the latter full of grace and truth. Even this response is a gift of God, "This is the work of God, that you believe in him whom he has sent" (John 6:29). Believing is witnessing to the Word with whom we abide and to whom we commit our lives. Believing is the life that leads to happiness in becoming children of God. Believing means above all living in the reign of God's love. There are several beatitudes in the New Testament that describe the joy that comes to believers. The Fourth Evangelist has only one beatitude and sums up how happiness comes to the dedicated disciple, "Blessed are those who have not seen and yet have come to believe" (John 20:29).

Believe in him whom God has sent.

Faith means acknowledging that the only way to encounter God is in Jesus—this is what it means to be a Christian. "This is the work of God, that you believe in him whom he has sent" (John 6:29).

Faith is not confidence, enthusiasm, or amazement in the power, miracles, signs, and oratory of Jesus—these are all stages towards faith, possibly positive, but certainly not enough. Faith is the total redirection of one's life to Jesus and to his new values. In practice, faith means discipleship—persevering fidelity to the life Jesus has shown us. It starts with call, election by Jesus, a commitment to mission and service in his name, following him along the path he marked out for us, and a willingness to join him in the passion. From Jesus' perspective, faith means a powerful involvement in the disciples' lives. So, faith is a relationship between disciples and Jesus, the former acknowledging Jesus as the Lord who heals, saves, and teaches them. Disciples also commit their whole person to Jesus as the one in whom they encounter God. Thus, it means adherence to his word and imitation of his life of suffering, poverty, humility, charity, and service.

Faith is a grace, an unearned gift from God that calls for a commitment that touches the depths of our being and personality. Even when permanent, it is always capable of increase or threat from sin. Disciples have made a commitment in faith, but that gift of God needs to grow. The fundamental redirection of our lives to God by faith in Jesus is only the beginning of an ongoing life of faith with its ups and downs. Deficient faith does not mean unbelief, but a commitment which has not reached its full potential. At times the disciples asked the Lord, "Increase our faith!" (Luke 17:5). On another occasion, Jesus replied to Peter, "I have prayed for you that your own faith may not fail" (Luke 22:32). Faith means receiving Jesus, knowing him, and acknowledging him as the one sent by the Father. It means giving our lives to Christ, accepting and receiving him, remaining faithful to his Word.

Integral to the dynamism of faith are four key concepts: hearing, seeing, knowing, and believing. Hearing means an attentive listening so that one can be taught by God and then be true to Jesus' Word and to the revelation of the Father. Seeing is the spiritual insight and vision that goes with faith and sometimes results from it. It is a different way of looking at reality. Knowing means personal understanding, experience, dynamic interaction, the daily learning of the impact and power of the life of faith. Believing does not mean intellectual knowing but an intimate acceptance of who Jesus is. This conviction, inner knowledge, acceptance, and wisdom is the faith that guarantees eternal life. "Do not let your hearts be troubled. Believe in God, believe also in me. . . . I am the way, and the truth, and the life. No one comes to the Father except through me" (John 14:1, 6).

Our journey of faith.

Faith is not an intellectual commitment to the Creed or to what someone says is Catholic teaching, and it certainly is not a requested dedication to a whole series of sexual-gender positions sponsored by one group or another. We can never earn faith by personal efforts, or by commitment to a checklist of teachings. Faith is one of Jesus' greatest priorities, one of the three great energies of the soul. It is a transforming gift of God that enables us to hear, see, know, and believe that all reality has meaning only when centered on Jesus. "Very truly, I tell you, anyone who hears my word and believes him who sent me has eternal life, and does not come under judgment, but has passed from death to life" (John 5:24).

There is always darkness in the journey of faith. It is not the result of accumulated knowledge, and so we have no control over the experience. It is not the work of the intellect but results from denying the intellect its own natural objects and launching into an unknown. It is a dark experience because we leave aside what we thought was the illuminating knowledge of God from our past life and bid farewell to former certainties and walk into the unknown. It is a dark experience because we no not know where we are going for we are being drawn rather than deliberately moving forward. It is dark because while we journey to the Father we do not know the Father, but only the Son. So, with all the good will in the world, we will still have doubts and little faith (Matthew 6:30).

Faith means we acknowledge that Jesus reveals the divine mystery of God's love and is our access to the way of life God wills for us. "Everyone who has heard and learned from the Father comes to me" (John 6:45). Commitment to Jesus in love and faith makes sense of life. It is a synergistic blend that leads to a new birth and a new outlook on life, when we see that Jesus' teachings are spirit and life for us. Our commitment in faith means a total dedication to Jesus who comes from God and returns to God. It means entering the kingdom, gaining eternal life, coming to the light, and being saved.

Faith is an action rather than a synthesis of doctrine. The evangelist John always used the verb "believing" rather than the noun "faith." So, for each of us faith is something we do—it is an active commitment. Faith is not the same as being a "practicing Catholic" or a "church-going Christian." A person can attend church and have little or no faith. Faith permeates everything a person does and is. Moreover, faith cannot be set aside while one is involved in business, politics, healthcare, or organizations of all kinds. The values of faith affect everything a person does.

Faith and its resulting spirituality are not equivalent to religion. In the cases of fringe religions it soon becomes clear they have nothing to do with faith. Mainline religions, with their frequent links to politics, money, and social agendas, can easily drift away from the essentials of Christian faith. The values and priorities of faith are generally made visible in worship. However, worship can often cover up with pleasant platitudes the central values of faith and help participants feel comfortable with themselves. Values of faith in varieties of Christian traditions are rarely separated by honest evaluation of Jesus' priorities but by other issues. Ecumenical divisions frequently portray an unwillingness to base one's judgment on Jesus' priorities. Once, when Jesus was talking to his disciples, he expressed the sadness he often felt. "And yet, when the Son of Man comes, will he find faith on earth?" (Luke 18:8).

Consequences of commitment to faith.

Discipleship is the only way we can express our faith. It is a gift from God to which the believer responds, "But to all who received him, who believed in his name, he gave power to become children of God" (John 1:12). The acceptance of Jesus in faith means not merely accepting his teachings but giving ourselves to him in complete allegiance, so that from now on we find our identity in faith in Jesus. With Peter we say, "Lord, to whom can we go? You have the words of eternal life" (John 6:68).

Faith is an experience we simply cannot deny. In fact, every day is punctuated with experiences of a realm of life beyond this one. We now live in light of faith, making decisions because of our awareness of life and values that give meaning to this life. We live in comfort and challenge all the time; in comfort because of the Lord's continued presence, and in challenge because of the new values he sets before us.

Some people unfortunately equate faith with doctrine, projects, practices, codes, creeds, or worship. Perhaps instead of finding people like those of whom Jesus spoke, "anyone who hears my word and believes him who sent me has eternal life, and does not come under judgment, but has passed from death to life" (John 5:24), he will find well-meaning good people taught by other well-meaning good people—all of whom simply made wrong choices and pursued the wrong priorities.

Living in faith means living in darkness. This is so, partly because we cannot see clearly in this life and must walk with courage even when we do not see the end of our journey. However, sometimes the darkness does not result from the absence of light but we cannot see because we are overwhelmed with the brightness of the presence of God—as if we are standing in the headlights of an on-coming car. Both experiences can be disorienting.

Living in faith means letting go of control over our own lives. Faith is the life of receptivity and gift and we can feel helpless, drifting a while without seeing the goal. But in the life of faith we are not moving ourselves towards a goal, but being drawn by a loving God towards our goal. Our task is to make sure we do not place any obstacles in the way of the growth God has ordained for us.

FAITH

Faith is a gift of God that enables us to understand our place is this world. Faith is a way of looking at reality, at the big picture of God's involvement in our lives and in our world. Faith means commitment—always acting in light of God's will for us in this world.

Questions for personal reflection or group discussion.
1. How do you learn about God and God's will for you?
2. What does faith mean to you? Give some examples.
3. What are the dark experiences in your journey of faith?
4. Does your local church community equate faith with doctrine or experience?

5. What are the consequences of knowing you are not journeying forward to God but being drawn forward by God?

HOPE-when all seems hopeless

The third great energy of the soul is hope. This also is a transforming gift from God. It is not the accumulation of small daily hopes every human being seeks to fulfill. Rather, it is a gift from God that totally changes the way we live. To live in hope, to be people of hope, makes life exciting, fulfilling, and worth living. "Now faith is the assurance of things hoped for, the conviction of things not seen" (Hebrews 11:1). People who live without the hope that motivates life become people of despair ("despair" comes from Latin and means no hope). So many people feel lonely, abandoned, and without purpose in life—they are longing for love, faith, and hope.

In hope we are saved.

Love and faith are two of the great priorities of Jesus' teachings. We hope for these gifts—we hope for love and faith. We also hope precisely because we have love and faith. If we did not hope for them, they would be merely empty words. Hope makes faith real because God is a God of promise. "May the God of hope fill you with all joy and peace in believing, so that you may abound in hope by the power of the Holy Spirit" (Romans 15:13). Hope is God's gift to us, or to put it another way, God is our hope. This gift transforms our lives, and while looking to the future it influences everything we do in the present and informs how we now approach God. Our future with God gives meaning to our present.

The accumulation of ideas from the past is not what motivates and transforms us but the vision of God's future. "For in hope we were saved. Now hope that is seen is not hope. For who hopes for what is seen? But if we hope for what we do not see, we wait for it with patience" (Romans 8:24-25). This is part of the experience of darkness that accompanies hope. Sometimes we think we see the wonders of God's love because we are comforted by the many ways God has been present to us throughout salvation history. But this is nothing in comparison to the wonders of God's vision of our future in the hope placed before us. "No eye has seen, no ear has heard, no mind has conceived what God has prepared for those who love him" (1 Corinthians 2:9).

Hope is the proof of our faith. Hope is about the meaning of life, about what it means to be human, to be a Christian. It is a daily conviction that we are being drawn to a new and greater reality, and this motivates us in all we do. In fact we live and grow in so far as we have hope. However, God's gift of hope is not the same as the desires we all have for self-betterment. These small or large daily yearnings and hopes are not the same as the transforming gift of living in light of the future. So, it is this gift of hope that reveals the greater truths about ourselves, and it also manifests to others what we love and believe. Men and women make their own end and purpose real in their commitment to hope. It is hope that helps us bridge the gap between this present horizon of life and the realm of life beyond this one, and this awareness conditions how we live in the present life in light of the future one. Hope reminds us who we are called to be.

Jesus proclaimed God's gift of hope.

Early Christians believed Jesus brought a new period of history. He insisted their hopes would be met in the kingdom of God which he inaugurated. This is more a reign or rule rather than a localized kingdom. Jesus presents it as future—realized in fullness at the end of time—but anticipated and imminent. Life in this reign of God is not earned but given to those who appreciate the centrality of love and wholehearted dedication in faith to God (Mark 12:34). The kingdom or reign of God had always been the object of people's hopes throughout salvation history, and Christians now find their place of hope in transformation by God. This is where hope is lived in the present. The parables of the kingdom show us that while this reign of hope is a gift, disciples' hope can be weak, can grow, and can become strong (Mark 4:1-25).

Jesus opens both his Galilean and Jerusalem ministries with the announcement that times have changed, people's hope is fulfilled, and the reign of God is here. The parable discourse gives us Jesus' understanding of life in the hope-filled reign of God. The kingdom refers to the future vision of God that comes to us in Jesus. Several parables give us a clear picture of this reign of God's mercy and compassion. The parable of the "sower" tells us how people respond in different ways to God's invitation. The "weeds" reminds us how hope-filled disciples live alongside those of no hope. The "mustard seed" and "leaven" describe the wonders of the kingdom's future growth. The "treasure" and the "pearl" confirm that this gift is worth any sacrifice we need to make. The "net" along with the "ten virgins" (and the "weeds") remind us that the reign is future—the fulfillment of our hopes.

God's gift of living hope is equivalent to living in the kingdom of God. This requires a conversion and a new direction in life—a total commitment to follow Jesus (Matthew 11:28-30). It will mean a new set of attitudes and a new lifestyle—all modeled on Jesus. Disciples will form a community of hope who live ready for the end-times. By living in the reign of God disciples become the community of God. Like love and faith, hope comes from God and is encountered in Jesus.

Life in the kingdom is another way of speaking about a new birth that comes from God when we accept the gift of discipleship. When Scripture speaks about "new creatures" it is referring to those who are filled with hope because they have the seeds of God's own life within them. So, the New Testament calls us "new creatures," and claims that as we struggle to discover our meaning and purpose in life, we realize that we come from a "new birth," a "birth from God," a birth by the word of truth (James 1:18). We are who we are because God has implanted a seed of divine life in us—this is the reason for our hope. Peter in his first letter concludes, "You have been born anew, not of perishable but of imperishable seed, through the living and enduring word of God" (1 Pet 1:22-23). John also tells us that we are begotten of God because God has given us something of the divine life (1 John 3:9). This gift of divine life is made to us in Jesus, the Father's only beloved Son. "For just as the Father has life in himself, so he has granted the Son also to have life in himself" (John 5:26). Being children of God is real not adoptive, we become children with the Son because we share in the same life. Thus, the triangle of relationships is complete; the Father, Son, and disciples abide in each other's love, and this love is the life of God. To be children of God means we share in the love of God and we come to know God in faith, and we long for life with God in hope. "Praise be to the God and Father of our Lord Jesus Christ! In his great mercy he has given us new birth into a living hope through the resurrection of Jesus Christ from the dead" (1 Peter 1:3).

We live in hope.

The writer of the letter to the Hebrews tells us to "seize the hope set before us" (Hebrews 6:18). The problem is that hope can fill us with suffering, as it did for Christ who had to face the cross to defend his vision of future life. However, we try to remain firm as "prisoners of hope" (Zechariah 9:12), ever ready to walk through the "door of hope" (Hosea 2:15). In implementing God's vision of hope we will need to face up to suffering—our own and other peoples'. We need to be firm in our expectation, courageous as we persevere in our hope-filled lives. Moreover, we cannot achieve the vision of hope on our own, but only together with like-minded others. So, hope calls for human understanding, solidarity, and compassion. In fact, hope is not only an expression of our faith but also of our love. As long as our yearning for God's vision does not transform the lives of other people then it is inauthentic. Living in hope transforms the present for the vision of God always includes community.

Hope is not focused exclusively on the future. Rather, it is a way of approaching the present because of what we believe about the future. So, hope is a very real aspect of contemporary life and not some naïve escapism into an unknown future. We realize our future, God's life of promise, in daily activity, when we make the future real now. St. Peter tells us to be always ready to give witness to the hope that lies within us (1 Peter 3:15), and we witness to hope by transforming the present into what God would wish it to be. Daily we live with a spirit of watchful waiting, gradually and incrementally fulfilling the vision of hope. We continue to hope even when life seems to have no meaning.

While hope can give us peace and satisfaction, it also frequently causes unrest when we look at the way things are. Christians cannot abandon dedication to the present because they believe things will be better in an afterlife with God. Our hope reminds us that our present life is in part an anticipation of life with God, and we strive daily to make God's vision a reality. Our task includes flexibility and adaptation as we try to balance the overwhelming love of God for the future with the fears, anxieties and yearnings of humanity in the present.

The only real question for human beings is what will happen at the end of life. The way we view the end in hope can revolutionize how we deal with the present. If we make the end time irrelevant, we make our lives meaningless and irrelevant too. We cannot hope when we always remain earthbound. Faith means being committed to hope. Hope becomes a way of approaching the present because of what we believe in the future. We live in spiritual tension between "the already" and "the not yet." "So, if any one is in Christ, there is a new creation; everything old has passed away; see, everything has become new!" (2 Cor 5:17). So, our hope demands that we live responsibly in the modern world. Nowadays, hope for the promises of God in afterlife has become hope for the world as an anticipation of the afterlife. Put another way, hope should make us creative in dealing with the present and challenge us to create a desirable future in the present, not just for ourselves but for others too, for hope is always a shared hope. Hope is a way of living one's faith and love. What is "there and then" inspires us to develop a "here and now."

Present consequences of living in hope.

People of hope are open to others, to new ideas, to diversity, and to change, always ready to listen, to learn, and to be enriched as part of looking forward in hope. They are people of humility since they appreciate that fulfillment lies in the future God has in store for us—so they have a healthy understanding of their own roles in the activities of the world.

People of hope are generally collaborative and dialogic, since they believe that God's future is being built up for us together in anticipation of God's final act of purification and transformation. So, showing respect for others' values, contributions, and opinions is all part of constructing a vision together. All this requires simple human qualities of truthfulness, gentleness, respectful listening, and mutual encouragement—exercised in families, churches, and political life.

Being hopeful also means guaranteeing other people's freedom so that they can contribute to the growth of the whole. When people's rights are denied or people's voices are suppressed in conversation, they cannot contribute what others might need.

Sometimes people are not free because of their own inhibitions, prejudice, ignorance, apathy, and so on. People of hope will struggle to help others free themselves so that they can be enriching components of community. Diversity and equality should be hallmarks of the human community.

People of hope are always people with a sense of wonder, awe, and mystery. They understand and appreciate that extraordinary things lie in the future. People of hope tend to train themselves to be inspired by the wonders of daily life so that they can see what others do not see, even seeing the presence of God's vision of hope where others do not. Thus, they see and create beauty as an antidote to violence.

People of hope are optimistic, joy-filled, and enthusiastic. They hope even when the immediate future seems bleak. They take a hopeful view of reality, expect positive outcomes, anticipate the good to which commitment leads. They are possessed by God—enthusiastic—(en theos) and enjoy life—savoring every moment and experience.

Working to implement God's vision of hope can also be filled with setbacks and failures. People of hope do not get discouraged as they work with incremental steps in the attaining of the vision for which they long. They need to constantly bounce back, find new energy, and move forward again towards the vision that entices. These people are capable of reinventing themselves in face of challenges. People of hope are also people of fortitude. They live hope with determination. It is a vision in the future that needs implementing in small anticipations every day, and this requires constancy, strength of purpose, and a generous heart.

HOPE

Hope helps us maintain our attention to the wonderful future that God has prepared for us and offers us. It gives meaning to our present life by reminding us what lies ahead. Hope is the most powerful motivating force for faith.

Questions for personal reflection or group discussion.
1. What is the difference between hope and expectation?
2. How does hope prove faith real?
3. How would you describe in contemporary terms the notion of the kingdom of God?
4. How does hope impact the way we live in the present?
5. Are you a hope-filled person? Give examples.

THREE CHALLENGES

At the beginning of the New Testament, John the Baptist challenged his listeners to conversion, criticized their lack of integrity, and told them that Jesus would call them to a new life in the Spirit (Matthew 3:7-12). This was Jesus' own mission among his disciples—to call for conversion, integrity, and life in the Spirit. These three fundamental challenges are now our response to the three transforming gifts that God makes to us—love, faith, and hope. While these three challenges are our responsibility, they are also God's work within us. God draws us to conversion, integrity, and holiness of life. Our dedication will need to be permeated with the four cardinal virtues. Fortitude is that courage and determination to persevere with our commitment—it helps us avoid all half-hearted dedication. Prudence is the virtue of exercising sound judgment in the decisions we make—it keeps all we do in perspective. Temperance is the virtue by which we govern everything we do with moderation—it makes sure we do not slip into exaggerations and fanaticism. Justice calls us all to treat everyone fairly and to respect the rights of everyone—it assures us that pursuing our goals is never at the cost of others.

These three challenges of conversion, integrity, and spirituality become life-changing responses that enable us to pursue the transforming life of love, faith, and hope that are God's essential gifts to us.

CONVERSION-in times of self-righteousness

Jesus put his greatest energy into challenging people to conversion—changing the minds and hearts of others through his ministry. It was the first topic mentioned by both Jesus and John the Baptist in their public ministries. It is the starting point for all other values or stages in the spiritual life, and one of Jesus' greatest priorities.

Called to conversion.

Along with the transforming gifts of love, faith, and hope God grants to each of us the call to conversion. The gifts and the call are simultaneous, even though a believer may not be aware of one or other for some time. In fact, letting love take over the emphasis of multiple desires, making faith the center of knowledge rather than the intellect, and allowing hope to overwhelm the accumulation of memories—this process is itself a conversion. Conversion means a change of heart, as long as we remember that in Jesus' time heart was considered to be the source of both emotions and knowledge—and so conversion came to mean accepting a totally new outlook on life. The new outlook on life centers on Jesus. Disciples who have a special relationship with him establish a fellowship among themselves in a community of followers.

Jesus always takes the initiative in calling people to discipleship and to the centering of life on him. He becomes our teacher, guide, support, and challenge. For our part as disciples we must repent of former failed choices, change the direction of our lives, dedicate ourselves in obedience to Jesus, build on his words, and accept the sacrifices of life in his name. The disciples' response to the Lord's call leads to the rejection of evil, painful choices, confession of the Lord, and a commitment to holiness of life. It also means joining the community of believers, publicly witnessing to the priorities of the Lord, and becoming salt of the earth and light for the world (Matthew 5:13-14). The disciples' commitment to Jesus has two phases—turning away from sin and evil and turning towards God. The former is often referred to as repentance and the latter conversion. True conversion is indistinguishable from discipleship. Those who accept this change of direction or change of outlook in life enter into union with Jesus that anticipates the future kingdom—an age of light, life, love, and truth. Disciples, drawn by the initiative and love of the Father (John 17:6), deliberately make the choice to live under the guidance of the Spirit and in light of the world to come. This changes everything for the disciple whose life is now totally directed to God (John 6:68-69).

Conversion is a spiritual awakening—an interior renewal—that challenges us to reject our false selves and false values and instead live by the values of the Spirit. So, it calls us as disciples to live on a new plane of being and actions, allowing ourselves to be influenced by God and by values of a horizon of life beyond this one. It is an opportunity to get to know God, while at the same time getting to know others and ourselves—maybe for the first time. This means that as disciples we live in opposition to sin in its many forms both personal and communal. It also means acquiring knowledge of God in Jesus Christ—again maybe for the first time. In conversion we find a new way of believing, living, and discovering that Jesus is the way, the truth, and the life. "Very truly, I tell you, anyone who hears my word and believes him who sent me has eternal life, and does not come under judgment, but has passed from death to life" (John 5:24).

Discovering the values of God.

Conversion is a radical transformation that implies breaks and separations from former ways of living and leads to living on a different level. Jesus required this turning of the heart from everyone, not just a select few. This is the way disciples live out the passion of Jesus, "always carrying in the body the death of Jesus, so that the life of Jesus may also be made visible in our bodies. For while we live, we are always being given up to death for Jesus' sake, so that the life of Jesus may be made visible in our mortal flesh" (2 Corinthians 4:10-11). Jesus considered that everyone needed to be called to repentance otherwise their hearts naturally focused on lesser values. This death to false values and resurrection to new life with God is particularly important today when men and women frequently seem to embrace wrong emphases in their lives. Everywhere there are signs of this drift away from values of the Spirit and towards a situation of disorder. Our lives ought to be God-centered but when left to ourselves we seem more frequently to focus on self-centered false values. These disordered approaches are produced by disordered men and women and seem part of a process of continual regression. Some of the worst disorders are those which have become imbedded in a culture and are considered the normal order of the day—e.g violence, consumerism, isolation, intolerance of differences. These are part of society, we think they are normal, and they are often justified by social and even religious organizations. At times the disoriented state in which we find ourselves paralyzes us, we cannot understand why, and our good intentions are insufficient to help us change. We ask God for transforming grace.

So many people today give the impression they believe that a person gets better by accumulating good things and practices—prayers, devotions, retreats, projects, ministry, movements, and so on. However, a person is not the sum of components—he or she does not get better by adding on or accumulating more religion. A person finds his or her authentic self by removing all the false approaches to life and finding God in the depths of one's heart. "Create in me a clean heart, O God, and put a new and right spirit within me" (Psalm 51:10). This is precisely what happens in conversion—the turning away from mundane values and the discovery that the new life God gives us is to be found deep within our own hearts. Peter, in his first letter, refers to the former as the useless way of life and the latter as a life when we become obedient to the truth. Paul, writing to the Romans, refers to the former as our imprisonment and the latter as the new spiritual way. In the simplest contemporary terms, conversion is a movement away from self-centered living, self-embeddedness, to self-transcendence.

Conversion is a process.

While essentially the result of God's transforming grace, conversion requires appropriate preparations and nurturing by each of us. Since conversion is a change of heart and outlook on life, it requires both emotional and cognitive preparations. So, we consciously or unconsciously prepare for conversion through open-mindedness and open-heartedness in study, discussion, and reflection. Moreover, in our preparations we can include new ways of thinking about the importance of community and appreciating others' gifts, contributions, and roles in shared values. Disciples' preparatory contributions will vary, but will always include love and knowledge—a changed approach to self and to others in community, and a change in one's vision and outlook on the world.

Conversion is a process. It starts with the preparations of new love and new knowledge. It gains focus through personal intentional reflection and group discernment. It finds nourishment in daily practices and in the implementing of changed values. It gains focus through the discovery of God's gift of life within one's heart. Conversion is never complete—it is the ongoing daily life of discipleship. It is less an achievement and more an attitude of reception and acceptance—an awareness of growth through letting go false values and allowing God to draw us to new life.

Conversion means letting God's gifts of love, faith, and hope have a transformational impact on our lives. Repentance includes abandoning false ways of loving, of knowing, and of remembering/hoping, and conversion means building life on new ways of loving, of knowing, and of hoping. In conversion we leave aside our self-assurance and allow God to take over the direction of our lives—God becomes our only teacher. This is a painful experience as we leave aside what we have previously valued. However, conversion is not just a change from sinful ways to morally acceptable ones, but it is often a change from false values—which we had thought were good—to new ones centered on God. This experience of letting go what we previously embraced can leave us discouraged and with a sense of failure at having spent our lives dedicated to the wrong priorities. As we move to new life focuses we can experience an underlying fear at the unknown future. However, only when one is emptied of false values can we be converted to new life with God.

Contemporary components of conversion.

A major requirement for conversion is humility. There is so much arrogance and self-assurance in our contemporary world, where people will not change for they think they are always right. They might actually think of themselves as principled as they cling to their ways of knowing and understanding life. Without humility, self-questioning, doubt, and healthy skepticism regarding one's own views, there is no space or opportunity for the kind of change that leads to conversion.

Conversion today includes the enabling of other people's conversion as well as one's own. The values to which conversion leads us are communal. Moreover, some of the worst false values that people cling to today are supported by communities, religious groups, and even nations, and so they need to be changed by organized confrontation—thus, the suppression of women's and girls' rights, the lack of healthcare, the treatment of the poor, the neglect of Vatican II.

Conversion is not just an experience that affects religious values. Rather, it is a change that affects the whole of life. Consequently it will lead to changes in priorities in family life, business, and politics. It is not just individuals who need conversion but entire groups, religious traditions, political parties, social and civic groups—to fight against oppression, the perpetuating of violence, the neglect of the poor.

Corruption is rampant today in all walks of life and has become one of the most serious destroyers of contemporary society. Conversion needs to take place in the hearts of those who are greedy for more of everything, even if it is at other people's expense. Businesses, healthcare organizations, financial institutions, government offices at all levels have been preying on the less fortunate, stealing the money they need to live decent lives. The greedy continue to ruin all levels of society and a few honest people must challenge them to conversion. Pope Francis' emphasis on the poor is a welcome change and called other groups to shift their emphases.

An area where conversion is desperately needed today is leadership. We have some of the worst leaders in politics, business, organizational life, and religion that we have had in centuries. Good leaders can do so much to transform the values of groups for the better, but we are faced with leaders who are criminals, profoundly selfish, and disinterested in their peoples' real interests and needs. Models of good leadership are few, and the affects of bad leadership are visible everywhere.

Conversion is needed in religion, the very place where one would expect to see it. Religious leaders are no better than any other leaders. In addition, so many of them are profoundly uninformed about theology and their tradition's fundamental values. They survive on fanaticism for projects and peripheral teachings while their people swallow up religious trivia, leaving genuine conversion out of the picture.

We need to stress that in conversion we are looking for the vision of God, no one else's. This means we have to find out what God wants of us and this will include reading, reflection, study, sharing, and prayer. Only genuine discernment can lead us to an appreciation of the vision of God to which we are called—that is the new outlook on life that we seek.

CONVERSION
We are each called to conversion, to dedicate ourselves to discover the direction of life that God has for us. This will need to be a carefully guided process that we approach with humility and maturity. Conversion is not a once and for all event but an ongoing experience that affects everything we do.

Questions for personal reflection or group discussion.
1. How have you changed in your approach to life in the last few years? Give examples.
2. Can you suggest two or three world leaders who have gone through a conversion? And two or three who should be open to conversion?
3. From which current ways of thinking or acting do you need to be converted?
4. Why do you think Jesus started his public preaching with a call to conversion?
5. How could your church change to reflect better the values of Jesus?

INTEGRITY-when we have lost respect for truth

Integrity is the spiritual discipline of always speaking the truth, of making sure we will do what we claim we will do, and of faithfully persevering in our priorities. Integrity must involve every aspect of our lives—personal, relational, organizational, and religious. It means accepting ourselves—what we have been and what we can become. Integrity implies that our core beliefs influence everything we do. What is within us affects what others see.

Jesus' principles of integrity.

The starting point for anyone who wishes to be a person of integrity is to reject the values of a condemned world. Jesus referred to the contrasts of two worlds as light-darkness, truth-falsehood, life-death. At times the differences between the two gives rise to a struggle for life or perdition. Many people prefer to live in the comforting values of a misguided world and reject those values that could give them life. Jesus said he knew what was in a person's heart (John 2:25), what attracts a person, what leads him or her astray. Jesus lamented that some people just have an inability to do what is right and instead of dialoging with his adversaries he bluntly confronted them. "I have come in my Father's name, and you do not accept me; if another comes in his own name, you will accept him" (John 5:43). He said some did not follow his teaching because they simply could not bear to face its challenge. "Why do you not understand what I say? It is because you cannot accept my word" (John 8:43). Even when the truth is clear some stubbornly refuse to accept it and instead choose their own false priorities.

During his ministry, Jesus encountered people who lacked integrity. He told them that words were not enough, but people had to show genuine goodness. Thus, acclaiming him as "Lord" was not sufficient, he expected obedience to the will of God. He told the crowds that they should give some evidence that they meant to reform, for he would acknowledge only commitment with integrity. Dedication to Jesus and the priorities he brings must be wholehearted—no one can accept him in private but not in public, nor have other loves more important than him, nor claim discipleship but reject the cross, nor try to pledge one's life to Jesus while trying to gain it for oneself (Matthew 10:33-39). Jesus rejected any half-hearted commitment. "Nothing is covered up that will not be uncovered, and nothing secret that will not become known" (Luke 12:2). Jesus told a story about a man who wanted to build a tower but never finished it, and one about a king who prepared for war and then abandoned it. He expected that everyone would follow up on his or her commitments. One of the saddest moments for Jesus was after the sermon on the bread of life when a lot of followers walked away and never returned to his company. Turning to his close friends he said: "Do you also wish to go away?" (John 6:67).

Jesus, like John the Baptist before him, launched some of his strongest criticisms against hypocrisy, especially in religious leaders—at that time the Pharisees and Sadducees. He also rejected any hypocritical show of religion—performing religious acts for people to see. Likewise, he condemned those who publicly give in charity so that others would appreciate their generosity. Rather, Jesus' approach was, "when you give alms, do not let your left hand know what your right hand is doing" (Matthew 6:3). On another occasion he focused on the hypocritical reactions of the self-righteous. "Why do you see the speck in your neighbor's eye, but do not notice the log in your own eye?" (Luke 6:41).

Jesus clearly appreciated integrity. He praised people who heard the word of God and kept it (Luke 11:28). He supported honest approaches to priorities of religion—even healing on the Sabbath, challenging the rules of hand washing as a sign of purity, confronting legalism regarding work on the Sabbath, and so on. He urged people to abandon the false securities of religious trivia to give priority to obedience to the word of God. Every day he calls us to separate the wheat from the chaff, reject what is not substantial and let all else blow away (Matthew 3:11-12).

The quest for integrity.

When speaking of integrity we mean only the integrity which is aligned to honesty and goodness. Evil people can show integrity in their consistent commitment to evil. Integrity is not a virtue we find in many leaders today, and this lack of sincerity, authenticity, and integrity makes many people think it is unimportant. Yet most people long to find it and expect to see it clearly present in the lives of those who claim to be Jesus' disciples. Personal integrity means being true to oneself in word and deed—an indispensable quality for people of living faith. Weakened or partial integrity damages one's ability to proclaim Jesus' message. Integrity includes speaking the truth with absolute candor and intellectual honesty. It includes consistency in dealing with others in light of our Christian priorities.

We apply the idea of integrity to someone who shows consistency between values and actions. People around a person of integrity presume they know the outcomes of their actions, for they think people of integrity are honest, truthful, trustworthy and reliable. Integrity is the opposite of hypocrisy. Integrity requires self-acceptance, truthfulness, fortitude, and inner peace. A person of integrity is one who manifests congruence between his or her inner and outer realities. Being true to oneself also means making sure that the organizations one belongs to are true to one's vision. On a practical level we will need to work hard for genuine integrity in our Churches and religious groups, especially following a decade when such organizations have shown a gross lack of transparency.

The Sermon on the Mount contains a large section on integrity and authenticity of religious values. Jesus proclaims that his disciples must not hide behind religious legalism but genuinely commit themselves to the inner spirit of religious values. He takes six commands of the scribal tradition and shows how he thinks they ought to be lived out. Jesus passes over all prior restrictive interpretations to get to the spirit of each one. Then Jesus moves on to comment on authenticity in religious devotions and in the practice of good works. He ends the sermon reminding his disciples to build their spiritual lives on solid foundations. Those who lack the integrity of spiritual commitment and thus lack solid spiritual foundations for their lives will find themselves up against a stone wall that formerly protected them and now will fall on them and crush them (Matthew 21:44). According to Isaiah, who is quoted in Matthew, God is the wall that supports authenticity and integrity and opposes hypocrisy.

Integrity is so needed today but there is a heavy price to pay for it. Following Jesus' challenge to their hypocrisy, the Pharisees began to plan his death. Jesus is seen in the gospels as provocative and at times angry with the insincerity and dishonesty he encountered, and his integrity made many enemies for him. Throughout his ministry Jesus experienced the hardships and brokenness of humanity—temptations, poverty, rejection, negative reactions to his challenges to society, Gethsemane, and the cross. However, disciples who seek to imitate his life of integrity are not only followers in healing and preaching but also in suffering. He told them that no servant was greater than his master (John 13:16). So suffering for Christians is part of the reality of seeking life—it means being willing to pay the price for one's priorities. Jesus knew the suffering that lay ahead for him, and it came because people were afraid of his message that rang with truth and authenticity, and they could not face it. Suffering is always part of the human condition—an ingredient that leads to growth. "Very truly, I tell you, unless a grain of wheat falls into the earth and dies, it remains just a single grain; but if it dies, it bears much fruit. Those who love their life lose it, and those who hate their life in this world will keep it for eternal life. Whoever serves me must follow me, and where I am, there will my servant be also" (John 12:24-26). Suffering is the proof of integrity—a disciple is determined to be faithful no matter the cost. Jesus is a pioneer for those who wish to live with integrity and authenticity, and he told his disciples, "If any want to become my followers, let them deny themselves and take up their cross and follow me. For those who want to save their life will lose it, and those who lose their life for my sake will find it" (Matthew 16:24-5).

Practices of integrity.

It is important that we always have a sense of pride in Jesus' message and the fact that we are his disciples. This includes being always ready to publicly acknowledge Jesus and our commitment to him. "Everyone therefore who acknowledges me before others, I also will acknowledge before my Father in heaven; but whoever denies me before others, I also will deny before my Father in heaven" (Matthew 10:32-33).

We should be single-minded in our commitment to Jesus' priorities, never watering down our commitment. We need to build our lives on the essentials of his vision and not on secondary issues. Jesus said that the pure in heart—single-minded people—would be happy and peaceful in life. Their commitment would excel that of others who divided their dedication on secondary issues. We need to evaluate our lives, careers, jobs, social involvement, political agendas, so that they are all part of an integrated dedication to our key priorities.

There should be no religious showiness in authentic discipleship. In the Sermon on the Mount Jesus condemned all devotions for outward acclaim. Rather, he insisted that each one should become salt for the earth by maintaining the quality of Christian life. When religion is often linked to social acceptance or to social agendas we need to be careful that we do not lose sight of our priorities.

There can be no distinction between our private and public lives and values. So we also need to examine both and focus on family as well as the priorities of organizations to which we belong. Business, political parties and Churches act in our name, and we must challenge them when their priorities do not reflect what we believe or what is appropriate to an integrated vision of life. We see people of integrity courageously challenge organizations or leave groups to live more authentically. We will have to tell some people that they cannot do what they wish in our names unless they share and portray our priorities. Clearly some so-called leaders in business, politics, and religion have lost the priorities that are important to us.

Integrity can be protected and furthered by our commitment to others in community. This means facilitating reconciliation with all around us, presuming their goodness, never imposing our own views, and fostering community discernment. At the same time we will put our priorities in the foreground, and so be realistic that some people never share the same priorities, and we can only go along with them up to a point.

Priorities are all part of a vision of love. We will always need to manifest our priorities in tangible expressions of love, so that our love is not merely a believed-in-love.

INTEGRITY

Integrity is the essential component of spiritual faithfulness. Jesus took every possible occasion to emphasize it and decry its absence. In our times, steeped as they are in corruption, superficiality, insincerity, and half-hearted commitment, integrity stands out as one of Jesus' most critical priorities.

Questions for personal reflection or group discussion.
1. Do others recognize you as a person of truthfulness, sincerity, and integrity?
2. Does your outer reality clearly and consistently portray your inner priorities?
3. Can you give three examples of people you know who are people of integrity and three who are not?
4. Could people around you identify your inner core priorities from observing your daily professional and family life?
5. What price do you pay for integrity?

LIFE IN THE SPIRIT-when others mock transcendent values

Spirituality refers to the human effort to become a person in the fullest sense of the word, to develop one's authentic self. It is the ordering of our lives so that we continually grow in positive ways. It embraces all of life, leaving nothing out, and makes us all well-balanced, well-integrated human beings.

Disciples' search for fulfillment.

One of Jesus' priorities was that disciples live a new life that would lead them to fulfillment. Along with New Testament writers, we sometimes refer to this life in the Spirit as holiness and sometimes as righteousness. Jesus told John the Baptist that he personally wanted to fulfill all the requirements of holiness. Scripture uses the word holiness—which means set apart—to indicate that disciples' lives are to be different than those around them. In his first sermon Jesus said that those who hunger and thirst after holiness would be happy, even though their commitment to the priorities of holiness would lead them to persecution. For Jesus this birth to life in the Spirit was more than outward practice of virtue or faithful obedience to ritual or the legalistic approaches of the Pharisees. Rather, he wanted his disciples to seek God's way of holiness before anything else (Matthew 6:33). Holiness is preceded by repentance and conversion to a new way of life. Its real starting point is an awareness of a new relationship between God and disciples.

God, the Father, the source of all love, reveals to us the divine will through the teachings of Jesus. Responding to the personal initiative of Jesus, the disciples' journey will be hard and filled with the challenges of the cross. However, faithful obedience to the will of God leads us to build a new world in faith, live in vigilant hope, and be always ready to be judged on our charity. As disciples we strive for the perfect pursuit of the will of God together with a holistic commitment to a covenantal relationship with God in Jesus. This relationship leads to holiness of life, shown in good works and justice, authentic relationships in matters of wealth, power, and sex, and constant effort to produce good fruits. Life in the Spirit is the result of the transforming relationship with Jesus. It is not something we earn but a way of life that he gives us. We must hold onto this gift and live out faithfully what we have received. It is a dedication to the Father's will encountered in Jesus. It leads to a new level of existence, new attitudes to life, and a new way of being present to the Lord and to each other.

What Jesus and New Testament writers called holiness or righteousness or life in the Spirit, we now refer to as spirituality. It was one of the great priorities of Jesus who presented this challenge to everyone without distinction. Admittedly, over the centuries, all kinds of distinctions and privileged groups arose to claim specialized forms of spirituality or to insist their spirituality was better than someone else's. What is clear is that Jesus' was a universal call for holiness in all his followers. Spirituality refers to the development of a life based on values, and Christian spirituality refers to a life built on the values, vision, and priorities of Jesus. Faithful following of this call from God in Christ leads us to self-fulfillment. This dedication also makes a qualitative difference in the way we behave in our daily lives, giving us values, vision, purpose, and perspective on life. Christian spirituality brings life and growth into authentic focus as it highlights the genuine concerns of life and human hope. It opens the way to the fullest and deepest values of human growth, the profound and intimate values we cherish most—the yearning for self-fulfillment, for love, for community, and for transcendence.

Christian spirituality aims to integrate the unique message of Jesus with the best of all human values and thereby produce a living synthesis of divine call and human response as they can be found in mature adult personalities.

When we pursue life in the Spirit we gain insight into the meaning of life, an understanding of right and wrong, and an awareness of the inner corrective challenges of conscience. At the same time, this spiritual life fosters a sense of mystery and awe, a feeling of security and peace of mind, and understanding of the afterlife and how it affects our current life in the Spirit. It gives us a larger view of life, a greater sense of freedom, and a realization of our place in history. Life in the Spirit allows a person who is in possession of himself or herself to celebrate and develop his or her own uniqueness. It is the most perfect form possible for self-determination and self-direction.

Some key aspects of contemporary spirituality.

Life in the Spirit includes an awareness of our call to continual growth in life by being dedicated to something or someone bigger than ourselves. This requires courage to be clear about our place in the world, to develop the best of ourselves, and to pursue our own originality. To achieve all this we will need to humbly leave aside the worst about ourselves, to be constantly self-critical of our lives and values, and to permeate our lives—especially in times of need and emptiness—with reflection and prayer. This life in the Spirit begins with an experience that calls for a change in the direction on our lives. It will be a contemplative experience that will emphasize the simplicity and intensity of the present moment. In that encounter with God we discover that our efforts are not the most important part of this experience, but rather what God is doing in us. At the same time this is not a selfish experience, for it will include a generous commitment to transcend self and become other-centered and God-centered. This means a concentration on unconditional love of self, of others, of the world around us, and of God. So, life in the Spirit includes the acceptance of our mission and destiny, our call and place in the plan of God.

Spirituality is rooted in a personal experience of God in faith which we then struggle to bring to birth in ever-changing circumstances of modern life. Faith allows God's power to transform us and to be fruitful in us. Spirituality directly connects with our human nature, making it what it is capable of being. It facilitates growth in life principally by purifying, directing, and enriching that life and not by sacrificing it or escaping it. Spirituality for a person of faith is the interaction of God's gift of transforming life with the efforts of the believer in concrete circumstances of history. Thus, it is always a transitory manifestation of perennial values.

Spirituality is rooted in the life of Christ which we find passed on to us in the sources of belief and religion, together with areas of contemporary knowledge that can enlighten spirituality, such as psychology, sociology, anthropology, and so on. Rooted in the great tradition of Christ's message, it cannot degenerate into religious fads while neglecting essential values of faith. Each believer, faced with his or her own emptiness, needs to be open to grace and to develop the faith-filled skill of waiting for God's interventions, together with an attitude of readiness to receive God's gifts and use them creatively.

Spirituality is a life of reflection and prayer. Prayer is a way of describing our God-directed lives. Growth in the spiritual life, seen as the life of prayer, is slow, and includes efforts to purify self, others, and the world of sin. It helps us face reality as it is, drawing fullness out of the present moment, deepening our appreciation of everyone, and developing a willingness to listen to all. It should also open us to every new dimension of our experience of God; and to root and celebrate our prayer in the worship of a loving community.

Spirituality includes a sense of humility, the humble awareness that Christians are not born as such, but struggle daily to become what they hear the Lord calling them to be. No period can pass without learning something new either in prayer, in sharing with peers, in ongoing study, in reflective application of the Word of God, in discussion with other believers, in the varied forms of openness to the many doers, thinkers, or teachers among us.

Spirituality permeates our commitment to every aspect of life. This results from us realizing that all life including our family and working lives with their new focuses of call are always a re-living of the baptismal challenge to belong to Christ, to live and love for him. This leads us to relate differently to self, others, and even the cosmos because of a new way of living our relationship to Jesus.

The service of others in professional life is a particularly splendid way of realizing this. We will need to renew this call on a daily basis, as we face increasing demands that must never lead to a reduced ideal of our calling.

Spiritual development only occurs with others. Those who can not share life or the service of others, or who can not cooperate or collaborate, or who can not celebrate together or build community together, are at an enormous disadvantage from a Christian point of view. Rather, genuine growth includes a letting go of selfishness towards others and self-pity toward oneself, and it calls for confident and courageous growth with others. Spirituality is directed to others in the essential Christian characteristic of service. The interaction with others is a way of embodying our spirituality in mutual service. Our love for the values of faith manifests itself in our attitudes toward others, not only those who are like-minded to ourselves but also toward those whose views differ from our own.

Some practical aspects of contemporary spirituality.

Spirituality is a call to become who we are capable of being. It is the way in which we can become our true selves in response to God's call, and therefore it cannot coexist with any kind of escapism. This will imply constant creativity rather than any acceptance of pre-packaged and recycled spirituality, whether from the saints of the past or spiritual movements of more recent times. We must reinterpret and adapt all these forms to our present life situations.

Spirituality is creative fulfillment not a battle against embodiment, and is only achieved through our embodied lives. Christianity does not morbidly focus on suffering and death but on growth and new life. Expressing our inner feelings through our bodies and rarely without them, our faith- and hope-filled love appears in a smile, touch, embrace, compassionate glance, weeping. Spirituality is not the discovery of our inner, spiritual, supernatural selves, but the directing to God of the whole of life. It optimistically stresses growth rather than a narcissistic focusing on our own asceticism and spiritual needs.

Christian spirituality presumes a positive approach to creation, whether that be the world around us or our human nature created and redeemed by God. Spirituality now refers to our concrete daily living when we deliberately try to make our faith real and effective on a day to day basis. Spirituality includes an ecological dimension through which we appreciate and enjoy the environment, learn from its balance and interdependence, and accept our role in it.

As contemporary Christians, we must be people who can collaborate with others in whatever common undertaking we share. Collaboration touches the core of a Christian's life, since it is not merely a way of doing things more efficiently but a way of being faith-filled people more authentically. Our contemporary spirituality will also stress an appreciation of institutions with their awkwardness and graciousness. Sometimes we will have to denounce the negative in institutions, even in religious ones. Always seeking to be holy and always sinful, religion will daily be something we can be proud of and ashamed of. In fact, an objective acceptance of the reality of religion is a sign of the maturity of our dedication.

We are dedicated to proclaiming the truth and need always to be open to search for that truth without ever absolutizing any channel or stage in the quest. Rather we remain ever open to the newness of God's loving presence and vital revelation. Our task is a prophetic one, to be a focus for honesty without counting the pain and persecution that this commitment now brings to anyone who challenges the increasing insecurity of the self-assured. This dedication to the truth means being a listener to the world—its political and social events, the signs of the times, people's hopes and joys, anguish and pain. All religious growth takes place in interaction with the world around us, amidst the trends and transitoriness of history.

Contemporary spirituality is a balance between selflessness and self-care—both go together and safeguard each other from unhealthy exaggerations. Rather, the generosity and enthusiasm that characterize a disciple's selfless service are nourished by time and distance away from the place and people of one's daily working life. Along the lines of self-care, our dedication can grow when strengthened by deep friendships, and for those who are married, by a deep relationship with their spouse—both relationships providing levels of intimacy needed for integral growth and a mature development of one's sexuality. Contemporary spirituality in public life needs to be complemented by a spirituality of intimacy. Deep, intimate relationships enrich our dedication by providing a core experience that not only nourishes, but also models love, community building, concern and service of a significant other which is the basic attitude of a disciple.

LIFE IN THE SPIRIT

There is nothing more important than spirituality which emphasises our fidelity to the inner values of our hearts and to our response to God. Spirituality will influence every aspect of our lives. It is that constant call to abandon ourselves to develop the priorities of God and to respond to the challenge of continual renewal in life.

Questions for personal reflection or group discussion.
1. What role does God play in your search for personal fulfillment in life?
2. Describe how you model your life on Jesus'?
3. How has your image of God changed in recent years?
4. Can you list four main characteristics of your spirituality?
5. Does your professional life reflect the same fundamental values of your spiritual life?

THREE SUPPORTS

Among Jesus' priorities we have seen three special gifts, three powerful challenges, and now we turn to three enriching supports. The Father draws us to new life and supports us every step of the way. The Son gives us the teachings that guide us and the love that nourishes us. The Holy Spirit calls us to fidelity to Jesus' teachings and is our daily Counselor in our struggles to be faithful in changing times. However, there are also three particular supports that are part of Jesus' priorities and sustain us in all we do. They support us personally and as a community and when we live them faithfully with fortitude they become supports for us as we live in a confused world in search of goodness and hope. These three supports are community, shared ministry, and universality. In community we find mutual love, shared vision, a common standard of faith, shared spirit of endurance, and joy, enthusiasm, and excitement for the journey. When we are immersed in a common sense of shared service, we enrich others and are enriched by them, we bring Jesus' transforming presence to the world, and we fulfill Jesus' mandate to go forth in his name. Universality is at once a mystical vision of God's plan for the world, it is a spirituality of daily involvement that brings the transforming message of Jesus to the world, and it sets Christians apart as people of universal love.

Jesus said he would not leave us orphans, but that he would be with us always, even to the end of the world. These three priorities of the Lord both challenge us and support us in fidelity to the call of discipleship

COMMUNITY—when self-interest prevails

Among the most important supports that Jesus offers his disciples is that of community. Part of discipleship is the call to the fellowship that shares the faith, hope, and love that Jesus brings to the world. Disciples are Jesus' own, the Father's possession, and they have new life in the Spirit. Their mutual love binds them together as the new people of God. Community is the concrete expression of their unity that manifests itself in love. When disciples are united in commitment to Jesus they are "one," as the Father and Jesus are one. In this section we look to how the followers of Jesus seek to show to others the mystery of communion that they live and how they find mutual support in the community of love.

Jesus calls his followers to build community.

Jesus is the good shepherd who gathers his flock together, and he is the vine that gives life to every branch in union with him. Life in the kingdom that Jesus brings is essentially a new set of relationships between the disciples, modeled on the union of the Trinity. Jesus is the essential embodiment of the new and true community. He is the leading lamb of the flock who sacrifices himself for the fruitfulness of the entire flock. Discipleship means following Jesus, but there is a wider concept of discipleship that means belonging to Jesus and belonging to each other in a mutual covenantal relationship.

Disciples were, and are, a core group that form a new community around Jesus. Always with him, they base their lives on his instructions, and choose a new direction in life to manifest their fidelity to him. They share together in prayer, fasting, purification, religious meals, and service to the poor. They see themselves as a pilgrim people, face up to crises together, live with vigilance as they await Jesus' return, share a common sense of mission, and reach out to minister in Jesus' name. Jesus refers to them as his new family (Mark 3:31-35). They share faith, live in mutual service, and purify their group from any scandal that can hinder its life. This community is not built on laws, prescriptions, and rituals, but on repentance, faith, openness to all, mutual service, and constant trust.

Following the Ascension of Jesus and Pentecost, the disciples' shared self-understanding grew, and they soon became aware of themselves as community. It was a community filled with hope. They saw themselves as a covenant people and appreciated that they were the mustard seed and leaven of which Jesus spoke. The prophets had foretold that part of the end times would be the establishing of the community of God, a community recognized by the great outpouring of the Spirit of God. In the experience of Pentecost the early disciples saw themselves as God's chosen people. Another characteristic of this early community, which they pass on to us, is their appreciation that they had a universal mission—to the Gentiles, to the ends of the earth.

The disciples became conscious of themselves as a specially chosen group—each one saved in the name of the Lord (Acts 2:38), called by God (Acts 2:39), and formed by the outpouring of the Spirit (Acts 2:1-4). Each individual finds that his or her calling is indissolubly linked to the Church-community. This belonging is not a once and for all achievement. Rather each one must remain in the faith, hold fast to the word (Luke 8:15), keep the word (Luke 11:28), and do the word (Luke 8:21). So the disciples are a community of ongoing fidelity to the Word and Spirit—open to the constant challenges of the Word, and ever sensitive to the continual and varied guidance of the Spirit. The fact we are all children of God should bind us together in unity.

Characteristics of the Christian community.

The Christian community is neither a place of refuge nor an institution offering ready-made salvation. It is a way of expressing our faith and commitment to Jesus. Our conversion is achieved within community where disciples believe they exist for each other. Here we look at four key characteristics of this community. Our modern day community, as an expression of one of Jesus' key priorities, will be a prayerful community, a sharing community, a poor community, and a joyful community. These characteristics give us all the support we need in living Jesus' priorities.

Jesus' life and ministry were permeated by personal, communal, and ritual prayer. He was a model of prayer, and his example stimulated his leading followers and local communities to become examples of prayer. They went to the temple, prayed in each other's homes, and celebrated the breaking of bread. Nowadays we all need to be everyday mystics who live with awareness of a life beyond this one and build bridges between the two through our prayer. Faith challenges us to be reflective and receptive, to foster an attitude of discernment regarding life's values and directions, and to be always connected to God through prayer. This prayer must be less about us and more about God. It consists in less words and more love. It always implies the search for unity among believers. Prayer is a gift, but we can prepare for it in four ways—develop stillness of body, learn to be inspired by the Spirit, train ourselves to concentrate with Christ, and immerse ourselves in the silence of God.

We read in Scripture that the followers of Jesus were of one heart and one mind (Acts 4:32). They seemed to delight in taking their meals together and sharing with others what they had seen and heard of Jesus. They shared their faith with enthusiasm and joy and extended this union to new communities that arose. This common bond of faith and love was seen in their practical sharing of welcome, hospitality, and encouragement in faith. The depth of their sharing was also seen in their willingness to share their material goods—as many participated in the collection organized by Paul for the needy in Jerusalem. In fact, we are twice told that in the Jerusalem community "All who believed were together and had all things in common; they would sell their possessions and goods and distribute the proceeds to all, as any had need" (Acts 2:44-45). We are also informed that "There was not a needy person among them, for as many as owned lands or houses sold them and brought the proceeds of what was sold" (Acts 4:32). When we look at the early Church we see many forms of sharing that gave them support in their discipleship. They shared instruction, prayer, worship, common property, meals, hospitality, and mutual encouragement in faith.

Jesus spoke often against the misuse of wealth and encouraged the renunciation of goods, almsgiving, and poverty. He was forceful against the accumulation of wealth, especially to the neglect of the poor. The early communities lived this in their commitment to make sure there was no needy person in their midst (Acts 4:34). So, becoming a member of the community meant removing need from others' lives by putting one's property at the disposal of the community. After all, Jesus had been very clear—

"You cannot serve both God and wealth" (Luke 16:13). Christian communities today can support each other in their prophetic stance against the consumerism, greed, and financial oppression that ruins people's lives. The spirit of poverty is the underpinning of all spirituality and is desperately needed today. Our poverty ought to be of disciples who are fully aware of our dependence on God. All else is human poverty.

It is interesting that in the New Testament we frequently find words such as joy, praise, glory, blessing, and peace. This is the atmosphere that permeates the communities of Jesus. Born in the Easter mystery, the Christian community has reason for constant joy in conversion, in faith, in prayer, and in outreach in ministry. In other words our contemporary communities of Jesus find joy and happiness in making a difference to other people's lives. We can be naturally optimistic and enthusiastic because faith gives us a new perspective on life and the future. We celebrate our own faith with joy, appreciate others' gifts and talents, can affirm the positive role of suffering, and in trust and hope contribute to the up-building of peace.

Community as a contemporary support of faith.

In spite of Jesus' hope that we would be a community of disciples we are mysteriously weak in building community. The hatred, divisions, polarizations, and partisanship that characterize the world in which we live can also penetrate into every dimension of religion. We need clear strategies to build community, for to be a Christian means taking care of others.

Jesus gives us the characteristics of community in his presentation of the beatitudes. There will be times when each member of community will suffer poverty, mourning, hunger, and persecution. Then there will be times when we must each be merciful, meek, single-hearted, and peacemakers.

Jesus ended his ministry telling the disciples that he would from then on call them friends (John 15:15). He went on to point out that friends lay down their lives for other friends. In our contemporary, anonymous world we need to build friendships as a genuine portrayal of Christian love and unity.

In his final discourse during the Last Supper the one great desire that Jesus prayed his Father would achieve was to build unity in the Christian family. Unfortunately, there is not much unity to be found. Our communities are full of divisions, different theological interpretations, different priorities, various social agendas, even racism, sexism, and all kinds of mutual oppression. Our Christian communities should not just be bound together by common religious bonds, but we must take care of each other's human earthly needs. This opens us to the challenge of social justice and of the fight against all forms of discrimination.

Part of being a community means presence and participation. We cannot build community without being present to each other and participating in common endeavors. Our community cannot be merely a Sunday get-together, but an experience of mutual love and mutual service. We need to share with those who hold different views and with those who have left the common community. We need to find modern ways of washing each others feet as a sign of our love.

Our communities must be filled with forgiveness and reconciliation (Matthew 6:14-15). Only when we have forgiven others can we ask for forgiveness for ourselves. We need to be at peace with ourselves and with others and to forgive ourselves and others. We should joyfully celebrate who we all are, our gifts, and our efforts to grow. We can never be controlled by structures, past problems, failures, or guilt. Reconciled with ourselves and with others, we build up the Christian community and then reach out to others beyond our own community to enrich them with our vision of the union to which God calls us.

In the Last Supper Jesus made it clear that one of his most important priorities was that he wanted to see union in the lives of his disciples—he wanted them to establish a communion with God and communion with each other. His disciples were to be a mystery of communion, an intimate communion of life, of love, of imitation, of vision, and of service. All this will require constant effort to build unity in thought, in common initiatives, in shared prayer, in planning, and in common pastoral outreach.

COMMUNITY
Being a Christian means centering one's life on others. In our anonymous and selfish world, we make this great priority of Jesus our own—to build community at all levels of our life. The challenge of faith is always to move away from self-centeredness to center one's life on God and on others.

Questions for personal reflection or group discussion.
1. What do you do to build community?
2. Do you find life-giving experiences on your own or with others? Why?
3. How do you show in practical manifestations your conviction that you share a common bond of faith with others?
4. What are the ways in which you take care of others?
5. Do you participate in common endeavors or do you prefer your own time and space?

SHARED MINISTRY-when many are so self-centered

Discipleship and the call to ministry go together. The same Spirit who calls us to follow Jesus also calls us to ministry in his name. Each one of us has been given his or her own share of grace, given as Jesus willed it (Ephesians 4:7). One of Jesus' great priorities is that every follower feels a summons to service—to live, to love, and to labor for the good of others. Faith never allows a passive attitude or a focus on self, but insists that the outpouring of the Spirit is always for the common good.

Companions who share in mission and ministry.
In the very first scene in which Jesus calls his disciples to follow him he also identifies their future mission as service to others. However, those whom he calls do not immediately rush off to work in his name. Rather, they spend time with him as companions in learning, sharing, and training. Only being with Jesus over prolonged periods of time qualifies people to participate in his ministry. In the

New Testament writings disciples are sent out by Jesus—hence their designation as apostles—to do two things, to proclaim the message of Jesus and to heal the world of its many forms of evil; in other words to preach and to exorcise. Apart from these brief experiences in outreach to others, the disciples' principal task is to remain in Jesus' company. Only after times in union with Jesus can they reach out to bear witness, to proclaim Jesus' message to everyone—even to the Gentiles, and to use all their talents for the benefit of the reign of God. The rabbis in Jesus' time used to gather their disciples around them to study the Torah, whereas Jesus gathered his disciples around him to prepare them for their mission. In the *Acts of Apostles* the early Church began the practice of baptizing followers "in the name of the Lord Jesus," a phrase which would be better translated as "baptized for the purpose of the Lord Jesus." Authentic discipleship results in service of others.

Ministering in Jesus' name led away from the acquisition of power to the selfless service modeled on Jesus' own ministry—he came to give his life in the service of others. Nothing about his followers should reflect wealth or status or selfishness, but only poverty, simplicity, and concern for others. Disciples need to be aware of their obligation to take care of others, to collaborate without vying for power, and to share ministry with each other. This ministry requires an enthusiastic acceptance of the cross, an imitation of selfless service, prayer, and confidence that Jesus is working through them. Those who minister in Jesus' name must be courageous, ready to accept persecution, and persevere with the fortitude of the prophets.

So, all followers of Jesus have a mission and a ministry as part of their solidarity with Christ. The Christian vocation by its very nature is a vocation to serve others—thus, disciples, as chosen partners, prolong and extend the work of Jesus. Mission and ministry are closely connected. Mission refers to the reason why people exist or are "sent." Ministry refers to services accomplished because of one's sense of mission. Mission is visionary, ministry is functional. The vision of mission manifests itself concretely in a variety of ministries. The latter then becomes a clear indication of one's sense of mission. The Father gives content and direction to mission, for it is his plan which is gradually unfolded by Jesus through his emphasis on the great priorities of his life's work. We carry out this mission when we are obedient to the teachings of Jesus.

Disciples, through their variety of ministries, manifest their sense of mission. These ministries are always centered on Christ and his values and vision. They are liberational—filled with compassion, as they free people from all kinds of ills of body, mind, heart, and soul. Disciples carry out this healing ministry aware of Jesus' compassionate, active presence to them. Ministries lead to the integral, holistic well-being of others through the creative development of new ministries to respond to new needs. The disciples' ministry is also a reflection of their community, justified by community, and a manifestation of its common values.

A theology of ministry.

It is interesting to read the New Testament, especially the parts written by the evangelist Luke, since he has a particular interest in the Church's program of ministry. He divides the gospel in to periods of ministry—Galilean, journey, and Jerusalem. Even the infancy narratives are a pre-ministry summary. Each of these periods has similar characteristics. Then in Acts, the first half consists in Peter's ministry to the Jews, and the second half is Paul's ministry to the Gentiles. Interspersed, we find the ministries of Stephen, Philip, and Barnabas. Whenever Luke uses the term "disciple" he means "disciple-minister." Luke's call to his community is a call to renewal through ministry. Disciples show their fidelity to Jesus by their involvement in ministry. Whenever Luke speaks about ministry he refers to the same seven components. His constant repetition of the same seven ideas suggests that this is Luke's theology of ministry—these are components he considers essential to Christian ministry for every baptized believer, and they remain a valuable reminder for us too. Every period of ministry begins with an episode that portrays a person's awareness of the call to minister to others as part of a sense of co-responsibility in the Church. He or she who ministers in Jesus' name always experiences rejection. Ministry is basically a prolonging of the preaching, teaching, and healing ministry of Jesus. In every case, the ministry is nourished by prayer, and it faces conflict from civil or religious authorities. Each period of ministry, whether in gospel or *Acts*, includes a sharing of ministry with others. Finally, there is no participation in the ministry of the Lord without a sharing in his cross. Luke weaves these seven theological themes throughout each period of ministry in gospel and *Acts*. His universal call and common themes offer us a concrete plan for pastoral challenge of all believers to participate in a contemporary renewal through ministry and to do so with enthusiastic dedication.

Our mission and ministry today consist in bearing witness to the great priorities of Jesus. Moreover, we do this with the same seven qualities Luke evidenced—a sense of call, a readiness to accept rejection, a commitment to the Word, prayer, acceptance of conflict, a willingness to share the ministry with others, and awareness that the cross is intimately linked to ministry. At times, we find good-willed people spending time in ministry on projects that do not reflect the essential components of Jesus' ministry, and more so, do not deal with his great priorities. Our ministry must be rooted in the essentials of Jesus' message, interpreted to make that message authentic in contemporary times, and open to the discovery of new ways of living the great priorities. Root, interpret, and discover— the three responses that guarantee authenticity.

Nowadays, increasing numbers of disciples develop a new perspective on shared ministry and the service of others. As more make this commitment, they find that they enjoy it and find it rewarding. For many it is an expression of their own identity. Two trends are identifiable—a growing awareness that service of others is an expression of one's baptismal dedication and discipleship. For others there develops a realization that in these years God is calling many men and women to make service of others a professional commitment. The former is part of the gift of faith and results in concrete attitudes of selfless service of others whenever occasions arise. The latter is a professional and permanent commitment to make shared ministry integral to one's life, often lived within Church structures but not always. There has never been so much emphasis on this great priority of Jesus as we have seen since the Second Vatican Council. At the same time we have witnessed regression regarding the teachings of Vatican II, an increased emphasis on clerical careerism, and attempts to push laity out of the roles they had gained since Vatican II. One of the results has been that many dedicated disciples have found extensive ways to serve within the circumstances of family, social, political, and working life.

Shared ministry in our contemporary world.

All religious groups set aside certain members to minister to the rest of the community in response to its internal needs. This is important but only affects a small group. The ministry and service disciples focus on today is that spirit of service that permeates the lives of all who are dedicated to the priorities of Jesus.

Christian service as a part of discipleship continually develops throughout history, and good people constantly discover new forms of expressing their dedication. To be an authentic expression of one's commitment to Jesus, ministry must not only embody the unchanging values found in Scripture—in other words be directly traceable to Jesus—but this dedication in service to others must also be relevant to changing times. As we serve one another within the community of disciples, we also reach out to serve others in need. However, we need to make sure that our form of service, done as an expression of faith in Jesus, is relevant and not just an expression of our need to be needed. It should include our appreciation of other people's spirit of service, so that together we serve the truth, share love, and serve the common good by our spirit of unity and shared service. Our service should be authenticated by the general acceptance and appreciation of the community, so that none of us becomes inauthentic or irrelevant.

Many people today focus on this priority of Jesus and together they can have a wonderful effect on the world and its needs. This spirit of service is a genuine vocation for increasing numbers of disciples. They see service of others as a personal vocation, and they learn the pastoral and relational skills needed in this service. The service of dedicated disciples reaches out to those in need, and the need is greater today than ever. Helping others growth in family life is a critical area—helping spouses in their relationship, guiding parents with the maturing of their children, bringing Christian values to all members of the family in their life together. Serving others to appreciate Christian values in professional life is desperately needed, especially when we have seen such extensive corruption and loss of other values in business, healthcare, financial institutions, educational institutions, and Church organizations. Christianity has always been known for hospitality, and today we see this service of others in our treatment of immigrants, people displaced by natural disasters or unemployment, and in welcoming home children who can no longer afford housing in troubled economic times. Christian service includes prophetically challenging failed political leadership, thoughtless wars with their death and destruction, and the ingrained bigotry of many political leaders.

Shared service is also important within the community of faith where disciples can enrich each other's understanding of faith through education, sharing, discussion, and common projects. Likewise, disciples strengthen each other's spiritual dedication through common prayer, community worship, companionship in the spiritual journey, mentoring and spiritual guidance. Communities of faith also have their flaws, and disciples can serve the community to growth by challenging abuses, correcting inaccurate presentations of faith, and insisting on appropriate planning for a vibrant expression of shared faith.

SHARED SERVICE

We are all called to the service of each other—that is how the human community grows. This was one of the three great enriching supports that Jesus emphasized for his disciples. His life culminated with the great mandate to his disciples to go forth in a spirit of service to the whole world, bringing his vision and values to all in order to lead the world to the transformation he came to bring. Disciples are not baptized for themselves but for the service of others in Jesus' name.

Questions for personal reflection or group discussion.
1. How have you increased your dedication to the service of others in recent years?
2. Does your service of others satisfy real needs?
3. How does the time you spend in union with Jesus improve the quality of your ministry?
4. Why do you think you were baptized?
5. How do you bring a spirit of service to your professional life?

UNIVERSALITY-when we fear diversity and stifle dissent

Jesus did not come from the Father to serve a particular group of people to the detriment of others. His concern was for everyone as seen in his daily lived conviction that every life was precious and that all laws must be secondary to compassion and love. He dealt caringly with people from all walks of life. To everyone he said, "Come to me, all you that are weary and are carrying heavy burdens, and I will give you rest" (Matthew 11.28). He was open to welcome all in the Father's name. "Everything that the Father gives me will come to me, and anyone who comes to me I will never drive away" (John 6:37).

Jesus' example of accepting everyone.

The early community of disciples soon opened its doors to all minority groups and integrated them into their common life in faith. They consistently showed concern for the poor and the oppressed, the outcasts of society and religion, and they embraced the new roles of women in Church and society. In his first sermons Jesus said that the Gospel was good news for the poor and the oppressed. When John the Baptist asked Jesus to clarify his own mission, Jesus replied, "Go and tell John what you have seen and heard: the blind receive their sight, the lame walk, the lepers are cleansed, the deaf hear, the dead are raised, the poor have good news brought to them" (Luke 7:22). Jesus welcomed and healed those whom society shunned and feared—the leper, the paralyzed and helpless, the woman with a hemorrhage, the widow of Nain, the prostitute, and Jairus' daughter. Jesus' attitude to the social and religious outcasts of his day is a perennial lesson for disciples in every generation. He deliberately chose direct involvement with those society shunned—tax collectors, Samaritans, public sinners. He even chose his closest collaborators from the poor and rejected. However, Jesus also ministered to the wealthy, privileged, and those in authority, never despising their position but always calling them to a sense of union and love for others.

Women were certainly underprivileged in Jesus' time, but he went out of his way to show special concern for them. In the gospels we often find that Jesus worked a similar miracle on two occasions—one for a man and a similar one for a woman, thereby showing their equality before God. For the third evangelist, Jesus uses women in his sermons as examples of the qualities he teaches—Peter's mother-in-law and service, the penitent woman and love, Magdalene and repentance, the hemorrhage victim and faith, the widow's perseverance, and the consolation of the women on the way to Calvary. Jesus willingly associated with women and knew their concerns and hopes. He had a close friendship with Martha and Mary, involved other women in his ministry, and gave a special place to Mary Magdalene in the proclamation of the resurrection. These approaches were readily picked up by the early Church.

Jesus' concern for all led him to condemn unjust social conditions. His teachings included a platform of justice and reform that challenged society's values and reaffirmed the importance of the poor and oppressed. For Jesus there was a close link between discipleship and commitment to social reform. He claimed that the absence of justice in one's life jeopardizes repentance and response to the Lord's call, for conversion and social justice are parts of one's dedication to God. Commitment to Jesus in faith overflows to others in justice and love, and this leads to peace. Universal peace was a gift of Jesus' ministry, for the salvation he brought resulted in peace. Those who came to Jesus and believed in him left in peace. This became so strong a conviction in the early Church that the very proclamation of the message was referred to as the preaching of peace for everyone (Acts 10:36).

Jesus gives us the example that our mission includes everyone. He emphasized this on the occasion of his encounter with the Samaritan woman at the well. "My food is to do the will of him who sent me and to complete his work" (John 4:34). Our vision of service must include the poor and the oppressed. It must draw through love the outcasts of every culture. Salvation is not for a few, nor is it truly religious unless it is total, open to the betterment of all and of every aspect of life, for the Lord's teachings also imply dedication to social justice. One of Jesus' great priorities was universality. Salvation for Jesus is integral and total. It is always a gift, and never earned, but we authenticate its reception in daily living. This daily living consists in a spirituality of universal salvation, a spirituality that calls us to live out the universal concerns of the Good News, welcoming all to the salvation which is Jesus' gift.

Our discipleship means being open to all.
Jesus was open and welcoming to everyone. He showed no discrimination to anyone who encountered him with good will. Appreciating this approach to God, Paul told the Colossians that God never favors one person over another (Colossians 3:24-25). In fact, Jesus readily broke down barriers towards social and religious outcasts. This is the plan of action for disciples—a radical response to the troubles of a divided, polarized, and embittered world. Universality is not a response to a problem or crisis. Rather, it is an awareness of a mystery of union, mutual inter-dependence, and reciprocal enrichment that is part of God's plan for the world. Universal love is the characteristic of followers of Jesus, and its absence is the single greatest indicator that someone belongs to the "world." Jesus makes it clear that all ethics and daily life are based on the command "love one another," and the theological and Christological reason is "because I have loved you."

Disciples manifest their convictions and values in interaction with people who do not share them. They live in tension—standing up for values that are different—yet loving all and rejecting no one. They are called to be the good seed that is mixed with weeds, or the good fish found in the same net as bad fish. Even when viewing themselves alone, they can remind themselves of Jesus' comment on the sower whose seed produces varied returns, thirty, sixty, or a hundred percent. The harvest will not come soon, and in the meantime the community of believers lives with righteous and unrighteous men and women. In this environment they live with patience, loving all, even their enemies. They model their lives on the Father's universal love, "for he makes his sun rise on the evil and on the good, and sends rain on the righteous and on the unrighteous" (Matthew 5:45). This leads us to live a theology of union with all, or what we might call a mysticism of universality. It is part of a new approach to life that illumines a world that otherwise lives in darkness. John speaks of this in his first letter. "Yet I am writing you a new commandment that is true in him and in you, because the darkness is passing away and the true light is already shining. Whoever says, 'I am in the light,' while hating a brother or sister, is still in the darkness. Whoever loves a brother or sister lives in the light, and in such a person there is no cause for stumbling. But whoever hates another believer is in the darkness, walks in the darkness, and does not know the way to go, because the darkness has brought on blindness" (1 John 2:8-11).

Jesus calls all to conversion whatever their background. He does not preach to a "remnant" as some of the prophets did. Although Jesus said that he knew what was in people's hearts, it is striking that he treats everyone open to the Word with remarkable graciousness. His approach did not always bring mutual appreciation and welcome. Some disciples left him after the bread of life discourse, others left after his cure at Bethesda, the crowds rejected his signs, and his own brothers thought he was mad. His opponents were untruthful, malicious, hypocritical, and sectarian but he remained dedicated to universal love. Jesus offers an enriching spirituality that affirms the dignity of every person as an image of God and as part of God's plan for universal love and salvation. This teaching often remains different from what so many would like it to be. People feed on discrimination, polarization, comparison, conflict, and even hatred. Jesus teaches by word and life the importance of universal love.

Jesus' death won for us all the freedom to love unconditionally everyone we encounter. This is the approach that leads to life. However, we need to remember that Jesus is both loving and just—he calls and welcomes everyone, but he exercises judgment against those who refuse to follow his path. To his disciples he says, "In the same way, let your light shine before others, so that they may see your good works and give glory to your Father in heaven" (Matthew 5:16). This is not a mission for a select few but a mission that is an essential part of discipleship. Jesus calls all those who follow him to go forth to everyone, especially the poor, alienated, neglected, oppressed, and broken people to bring a message of universal divine love. Universal love is not measured by the character or response of others—it strives for completion and perfection, a worthy reflection of God's love.

A spirituality of universality.

Universality means that the Father's love is given to all, that Jesus' mission is to bring a new vision of life to everyone, that discipleship calls for universal love and understanding. This commitment becomes our spirituality. It is not just a practical outlook on life or a vision of social interaction. It is a mystical-religious vision and challenge regarding what is God's plan for the world. It is a spirituality because we must find a way to express this vision in our daily activities. Discipleship means working to bring about the reign of God's love throughout the world. This means transcending particularity where groups or individuals act or even think of themselves as better, purer, more informed or enlightened, closer to God, than others. Disciples may well think of themselves as blessed, but so too is everyone else—the task is to find out how and then appreciate it and them.

Universality means mutual mercy and compassion. It was in the context of universal mutual forgiveness that Jesus warned his hearers that God would treat them just as they treat others. "So my heavenly Father will also do to every one of you, if you do not forgive your brother or sister from your heart" (Matthew 18:35). This vision of universal mercy and compassion shows itself particularly well in a spirit of anticipatory benevolence—we wish people well before we even meet them. Too often nowadays people approach others with preconceived ideas about them and what they think or who they are. We do this in politics, business, and religion. We do not give people a chance—we label and condemn them without us ever getting to know them. Universality refuses to approach the world in this way. Our mercy and compassion towards others should be transforming of our own inner life. Rejection of mercy to others undoes God's mercy towards us.

There are two kingdoms in this world, but they are not made up of us and them. The two kingdoms are based on light/darkness, love/hatred, union/division, other-centered/self-centered, and universality/particularism. This is the way, the truth, and the life of which Jesus spoke. Disciples are dedicated to build this world of light, love, union, other-centeredness, and universality. This priority of Jesus is evident on every page of the gospels—God loves the world and sent his only Son to save everyone. Not all will accept, but universal salvation is the message of both Jesus and disciples everywhere.

Contemporary society loves divisions. Foolish political leaders build walls to separate people, ideas, families, ideologies, and religions. Societies are addicted to denying people equality for any and every reason they can think of. We have divisions based on sexism, ageism, elitism, clericalism, and nationalism. People establish biases and oppression based on gender, status, financial well-being, religiosity, and political affiliation. While we are overwhelmingly successful in dividing and polarizing people, we seem unskilled in building unity and in appreciating universality. As disciples we need to work for universal peace and challenge people to work for peace, remembering the words of the Book of Proverbs: "the one who rebukes boldly makes peace" (Proverbs 10:10).

Our efforts to develop a spirituality of universality should challenge us to examine structures of oppression and discrimination. These structures perpetuate inauthentic human existence built on privilege, power, authority, wealth, education, and status. We must insist that contemporary structures—especially those in which we participate—be focused on anti-discrimination and on the enrichment of universal acceptance and respect. As soon as we criticize such structures we will become the object of their oppression. But, disciples must persevere with fortitude and even endure persecution to promote the vision of universality. In doing so, we must not retaliate against our persecutors. "But I say to you, Love your enemies and pray for those who persecute you" (Matthew 5:44).

UNIVERSALITY

Our contemporary world desperately needs people who will live a spirituality of universality. We need to reclaim the Christian challenge of universality—striving to understand, accept, share vision, dialogue with, and love all. When we do this, we find strength and support for our own commitment to universal love and acceptance.

Questions for personal reflection or group discussion.
1. What do you think were Jesus' priorities in dealing with the people he met?
2. In what ways do you think disciples today are persecuted for their commitment to universality?
3. What are today's "isms" that destroy universality?
4. What does "a spirituality of universality" mean to you?
5. How do you think the kingdom of light and love should focus its efforts today?

ONE GOAL: TRANSFORMATION—when we seek control

Jesus came from the Father filled with enduring love. He insisted that his goal among us was to bring us fullness of life, which means fullness of love. Now for each of us, the primary purpose of human development is to prepare ourselves for union with God, and we can never be satisfied unless and until we are filled with divine life in loving union. This is the transformation Jesus brings, and this is the transformation we need and seek. We will always be restless until we rest transformed in the love of God and until we discover our need in community of mutual love.

The goal of transformation.

God sent the Son into the world not to condemn it but to transform it. He came to open a new door in front of us, to travel by our sides, to guide us into a new future of mutual responsibility, harmony, forgiveness, and love. He gave us the outline of a new reign of God, offered himself as the Lamb of God who brought liberation, and drew near to us as the giver of peace. When he left us, he left with us the Spirit that gives life (John 6:63), as our teacher of faith, source of love, and guide to hope. Through his saving death and resurrection, Jesus gave life to us all as new creatures. He now thinks in us, wills in us, and acts in us, making every aspect of our lives fruitful. Through his resurrection we gain a new mode of existence, being transformed by the power of the Holy Spirit into children of the Father. The Holy Spirit is now active in us and in the whole world, leading us to the transformation God gives.

Jesus gave us his word that hovers over us like it did over the world at the beginning of creation. Through his death and resurrection Jesus raises us up with himself and we are all made new according to God's will and enabled to reach our authentic fulfillment. We become children of God together with Jesus, God's only Son. In this transformation we receive new clean hearts, and live in the constant presence of the Spirit. As Christians, we answer a call to be different, to approach life differently, to let God work in and through us, and to be motivated by a new set of priorities in all we do.

One of the most important components of our transformation is God's impact on our lives by means of the three theological virtues. By re-directing intellect, memory, and will to their God-directed objects of faith, hope, and love, God enables us to reach our full potential. These three great energies that God places within us enable us to become who we are capable of being, reaching our full potential in lives given to God. Along with these three gifts Jesus also includes among his great priorities three challenges to which we respond with his help. We must respond to the call to conversion, to live with integrity, and to give our lives over to the guidance of the Spirit. In this life of faithful response God gives us three supports that are at the same time further challenges—community, mutual service and universality. So, this transformation that God brings is what our spiritual journey is all about—a re-living of Jesus' priorities, a striving for knowledge of and hope in God permeated with love. This is a journey in which we come to realize that God has already always been with us and one in which God draws us to divine life in deepening love, drawing us towards union in divine life. It is more foundationally about God's love for us rather than our love for God—we simply accept God's transforming love in our lives.

Our response to the gift of transformation.

We often live an illusion that the life we are living is all there is. However, if we wish to be disciples of Jesus, we must get ready for a call we never thought we would receive. Our lives must be built on Jesus' priorities, and we should become aware that the human search for fullness of life is found in God alone. This is the call to transformation. We all struggle with our personal pain and longing to be who we are called to be—to be our best selves. We achieve this fully by courageously pursuing the great priorities of life that Jesus gave us. In doing so we will discover God, and we will also discover ourselves. This journey will always imply collapsing habits from the past, living in faith, abandoning what we previously thought worked and now know does not, and journeying to the unknown, emphasizing Jesus' great priorities.

We can make this journey with confidence for it is not our arduous undertaking, scrambling to take a few steps forward. Rather, we are being drawn by the love of God. We must match God's gift of selfless love with our own choice to focus exclusively on a life of love. This transformation is God's work, and we surrender to the divine action within us. We cannot achieve it, but we can prevent it from happening by emphasizing the wrong priorities. There is only one major commitment that a human being can make, to pursue a life of love with the knowledge that nothing else matters.

Our commitment begins with the realization of our call, and we must deliberately reflect on this awesome reality. We have a personal calling to union with God in love. If we have not thought of this before, then it implies a new perception of our life, identity, and destiny. To strive for union in love is our enduring purpose in life, and this is what must motivate us in all we do. This sense of identity and enduring purpose comes from the inward journey into our heart to discover our hopes, dreams, and deepest longings. It demands the capacity to be alone in contemplative reflection, to confront our perceived limitations and our willingness to be too easily content with a half-hearted response. We are asked to think about our spiritual calling in a totally different way, and this will always require humility at the greatness God has placed before us. Ultimately, spiritual growth is what God is doing in us, and so we will need to appreciate the sense of mystery of our life and surrender to this invitation. Above all we must never give in to a reduced ideal of our calling. We must be totally committed to the pursuit of Jesus' priorities.

Results of this transformation.

A first result of this gift of transformation is that we desire to make different choices than we used to. "So if you have been raised with Christ, seek the things that are above, where Christ is, seated at the right hand of God. Set your minds on things that are above, not on things that are on earth" (Colossians 3:1-2). We need to do what John called gathering the fruits of eternal life (John 4:36). In practical terms this means a total commitment to the pursuit of the priorities of Jesus—a different awareness of the importance of faith.

We appreciate that we are healed amid all our sinfulness and that we live in the presence of God's redemptive grace. We are no longer helpless as we face the world's hopelessness but can live in hope of change and renewal. This sense of healing extends to life in community in its various forms. God's healing and redemptive grace brings renewal to our efforts to build a community worthy of the hopes Jesus expressed

Transformation leads us to long to be obedient to the word of truth. "Those who love me will keep my word, and my Father will love them, and we will come to them and make our home with them" (John 14:23). This transformation of which we speak brings anointing and special knowledge to guide our lives. "But you have been anointed by the Holy One, and all of you have knowledge. . . . As for you, the anointing that you received from him abides in you, and so you do not need anyone to teach you. . . . But as his anointing teaches you about all things, and is true and is not a lie, and just as it has taught you, abide in him" (1 John 2:20-21, 27).

A further result of transformation is that we welcome the Holy Spirit into our lives. After the departure of Jesus, the Holy Spirit continues the guidance of disciples. "But the Counselor, the Holy Spirit, whom the Father will send in my name, will teach you all things and will remind you of everything I have said to you" (John 14:26). Because of this the disciples can live in peace, untroubled and unafraid (John 14:27)—calm in the certitude of the Spirit's presence.

In this transformation we feel loved and long to love others. One of the special characteristics of this change is the mutual presence and deepening of love between disciples and Jesus. "Whoever has my commands and obeys them, he is the one who loves me. He who loves me will be loved by my Father, and I too will love him and show myself to him" (John 14:21). Beyond this deeper love, the Father offers participation in divine life. This is not just something individual but is a participation that includes union within the community of disciples, the mystical body of Christ. So, this transformation includes striving for unity. "I tell you the truth, if anyone keeps my word, he will never see death" (John 8:51).

Part of this transformation is the intense desire to be faithful to our calling in the practical dedication of each day. Our faithfulness leads to this desire to prove our gratitude for the gifts of love, faith, and hope, to joyfully celebrate the life enriching challenges of conversion, integrity, and life in the Spirit, and to enthusiastically welcome the great supports of community, mutual service, and universality.

Above all transformation calls us to reinterpret what it means to be a Christian. We need to leave aside the many secondary, not to say trivial aspects of contemporary religious dedication, and return to an emphasis on the great priorities of Jesus' original message.

TRANSFORMATION

Our spiritual journey is one towards transformation—it is filled with our efforts, supported by God's grace—to become our best selves. There are innumerable spiritual programs to help get us there. There is a short cut which has two features: 1. we should decrease our own action filled efforts and let God draw us forward to union. 2. we need to focus all our attention on the essentials of the journey, those great priorities that Jesus stressed as the most essential qualities needed for this journey.

Questions for personal reflection and group growth.
1. How often do you focus on the goal of your spiritual journey?
2. Which aspects of your life do you hope Jesus will transform?
3. If you could change some components of your current journey to God what would they be?
4. How can you prepare yourself for transformation?
5. Which of Jesus' priorities do you need to give most attention to?

CONTEMPORARY SPIRITUALITY FOR CHRISTIAN ADULTS

Embrace the new enthusiasm in the Church and nurture your Christian commitment with just ten minutes of reflection a week.

A new spirit is stirring in the Church. We must overcome the failures of the past and prepare ourselves for a future of growth and responsibility. Let us rekindle spiritual insight, accept our spiritual destiny, and refocus on the essential teaching of salvation. While many have left the institutional churches, and sadly may never return, perhaps the challenge to renewal of Pope Francis may re-attract them to the essentials of Christian commitment. The Church will grow and benefit from an informed laity who deepens knowledge of the essential teachings of faith.

I created a book with short sections, targeting areas of personal reflection valuable for individuals and discussion groups for this purpose. Read a section each week and gain a new strategy for nurturing your spiritual life. Spend just ten minutes a week on the strategies -- in prayer, in discussion with others, and in living an enthusiastic, contagious faith.

Ten Strategies to Nurture Our Spiritual Lives: Don't stand still—nurture the life within you.

This book presents ten key steps or strategies to support and express the faith of those individuals who seek to deepen their spirituality through personal commitment and group growth. These ten key components of spirituality enable dedicated adults to bring out the meaning of their faith and to facilitate their spiritual growth. It offers a program of reflection, discussion, planning, journaling, strategizing, and sharing.

All books available at Amazon.com

Spirituality and leadership blog
leonarddoohan.wordpress.com

Spirituality and John of the Cross blog
johnofthecrosstoday.wordpress.com

More about all my books
leonarddoohan.com

www.ingramcontent.com/pod-product-compliance
Lightning Source LLC
Chambersburg PA
CBHW071408040426
42444CB00009B/2149